UNDERSTANDING

EQUINE
LAMENESS

YOUR **GUIDE** TO HORSE HEALTH
CARE AND MANAGEMENT

ISBN 0-939049-94-5

Printed in the United States of America
First Edition: March 1998
1 2 3 4 5 6 7 8 9 10

UNDERSTANDING

EQUINE
LAMENESS

YOUR **GUIDE** TO HORSE HEALTH
CARE AND MANAGEMENT

By Les Sellnow
Foreword by A. Gary Lavin, VMD

The Blood-Horse, Inc. Lexington, KY

Other titles offered by
The Horse **Health Care Library**

Understanding EPM

Understanding Equine First Aid

Understanding The Equine Foot

Understanding Equine Nutrition

Understanding Laminitis

Contents

FOREWORD

The horse or pony of any breed has been bred for centuries to achieve certain performance requirements. A Welsh pony or a Clydesdale draft and all those breeds in between, from birth and growth through their respective occupational lives, will be confronted with various lamenesses or unsoundness. It is imperative to their livelihood and sometimes even their very survival that we, their caretakers, understand at least some basic principles of lameness.

A basic knowledge of anatomy, particularly the skeletal and muscular systems, is paramount to understanding locomotion and athletic process. Many injuries, externally and internally induced, are common to any type of equine. Some injuries are peculiar to certain breeds and their activities.

Ownership of a horse requires a responsibility for its well-being. In return, the horse ultimately will become the teacher rather than the pupil. Beyond the obvious pleasure and satisfaction of participating in the world of the horse, the owner or rider will be taught discipline, patience, teamwork, compassion, and humility. As Will Rogers said, "There's nothing better for the inside of a man than the outside of a horse."

With the aforementioned knowledge of some anatomy, *Understanding Lameness* offers an entry level overview to the lameness problems of the horse which hopefully will unravel some of the many causes of unsoundness.

The reader should not be intimidated by what, at first blush, appears to be such a confusing and complicated subject. Any athletic endeavor will, from time to time, present obstacles that require attention and remedy; many are short-term and easily resolved. The help of knowledgeable horsemen, both amateur and professional, is always easily obtained. Horsemen stand united in their concern for the well-being of their equine partners and will most eagerly offer their best and lifelong knowledge to those who seek it. Don't hestitate to avail yourself of their services.

A. Gary Lavin, VMD
past president, American Association
of Equine Practitioners
member, Keeneland Sales inspection team

INTRODUCTION

There is no one single lameness expert. Instead, there are a large number of researchers and practitioners who have worked diligently through the years to put together this rather complicated jigsaw puzzle that we call *Understanding Lameness*. Some are farriers, horse trainers, and other knowledgeable laymen. Others are veterinarians and university researchers.

I have drawn on their recorded experiences, research, and reports with this goal in mind: to present material that will help the average horse owner better understand what lameness is all about and what can be done to prevent it.

Lameness is defined as an altered or asymmetric gait and it can have myriad causes. Lameness can stem from trauma, such as an injury to the horse's foot or leg. A horse can get hurt by tangling with a barbed wire fence, stepping on a nail, or stumbling in a prairie dog hole while on a trail ride. Lameness can develop because of over-extertion during exercise or competition. A tiring horse might take a bad step or rap a leg on a jump. Poor hoof care can lead to lameness as well.

Lameness can develop because of conformational faults. Crooked legs or bad feet can be passed down from one generation to the next, with sons, daughters, grandsons, and granddaughters developing the same lameness problems which afflicted their parents and grandparents. When horse owners make breeding decisions based on economics, fashion, or pedigree, horses with poor conformation and subsequent lameness problems can result.

Lameness can vary in degree depending on the cause. A horse which catches its leg in a fence or steps on a nail might suffer pain so severe that it bears weight on only three legs. Diseases of the foot, such as laminitis or navicular disease, also can cause extreme pain. But sometimes, the underlying cause of lameness might be so subtle that even a veterinarian has difficulty identifying it using nerve blocks.

Some lameness problems can be fixed with a few days of stall rest. Other lameness problems can mean the end of a horse's career, whether the horse is competing on the racetrack or being used only for casual trail rides.

Every horse becomes lame at one time or another and everyone who owns or works with horses copes with equine lameness problems. But horse owners can reduce the risk of lameness with common sense and judicious care. Owners also can compensate, to a degree, for a horse's poor conformation with proper shoeing and appropriate use. If, for example, a horse is obviously offset in the knees, it might become lame if it is put through the rigors of jumping high fences. The same horse might not develop lameness problems if used only for casual trail riding over forgiving terrain. But the basic problem remains and poor conformation ultimately can lead to lameness.

There is another facet to lameness problems that adds to their complexity — people often ask their horses to do far more than nature intended. For example, a horse normally will not jump over an obstacle unless there is absolutely no way to go around it. A racehorse competing over many seasons can suffer wear and tear, especially to the left foreleg, which can lead to lameness. Even a horse with good conformation can develop soundness problems because of excessive performance stress placed upon it.

Understanding Lameness provides basic information on the construction of the horse's limbs and describes the lameness problems likely to occur as a result of poor conformation. It explains how basic lameness problems can arise, then describes what can be done about them, and advises on ways to prevent some lamenesses.

CHAPTER 1

Forward Locomotion

Horses must move forward to be useful to man. That is a fairly basic and simple statement, but it neatly sums up a horse's purpose in life, whether the animal is used as a trail ride mount, a jumper, dressage contestant, or racehorse. If the horse can't or won't move forward, it is of little or no use to us.

Moving forward takes varied forms, depending on the discipline involved. A trail horse might never do much of anything except move at a walk, while a five-gaited Saddlebred will be asked to go forward at five specific gaits.

Obviously, different gaits produce varied stresses on the limbs, especially the front legs. For example, a jumper soaring over a five-foot fence puts great stress on the forelimbs when it lands. Cutting and reining horses put heavy stress on their rear limbs as they slide to stops, spin, and quickly change direction. A young racehorse, often competing on fragile legs, puts tremendous pressure on its limbs. At a gallop, its entire weight comes bearing down on one outstretched foreleg during each stride.

Where we ride or drive and what we ask of the horse, as well as its genetic makeup, will determine which gaits the animal must use. For instance, no one should take a three-gaited Saddlebred, shod for the show ring, and ask it to negotiate a rocky mountain trail at a trot. Nor should a rider take a sedate trail horse and ask it to perform in the three-gaited class in a show ring. Regardless of the gait required, our goal is to be mounted on a horse that will move forward and still remain sound.

Let's take a look at the various gaits listed below:

Walk — The walk is a four-beat gait with legs rising and falling at separate intervals. All horses walk and when they do, at least two of the feet are on the ground at any instant.

Trot — The second basic gait of the horse is the trot. This is a two-beat gait with left front and right rear striking the ground at the same time, followed by the right front and left rear touching down at the same time. Between each sequence there is a brief moment of suspension when no legs are on the ground. It is at the trot that conformational defects in the legs often surface.

The trot.

Canter or Lope — From the trot, the horse moves a bit faster. This gait is called the canter by English-oriented riders or the lope by Western riders. It is a three-beat gait which can be described as a collected or restrained gallop. If a horse is traveling to the left, it will push off into the lope with its right rear leg, followed by the left hind, right front, and then left front. This is referred to as being on the left lead with that forelimb reaching farther forward than the right front leg.

Gallop — The canter or lope is not all that stressful, although it is up the stress scale a notch from the trot. The major stress

comes when a rider speeds up the process and the horse goes from a lope or canter into a full gallop or run. The gallop has a four-beat pattern. When the horse is on the left lead, it pushes off with the right hind leg, followed by left hind, the right front, then the left front. There is a brief period of suspension when all four legs are off the ground.

The gallop.

At one point in every galloping stride, the entire weight and force of the horse's body comes to bear on the leading front leg. As a result, the leading foreleg will tire more quickly than the other three and always is at the greatest risk of sustaining injury. The veteran racehorse will switch leads at some point in the race, frequently at the head of the stretch, to ease the stress on that leading leg.

As we will see as we continue, good conformation in the form of well-constructed and durable legs is a must for equine competitors if they are to remain sound.

OTHER GAITS

There are a variety of other gaits, some of which are exclusive to particular breeds. They include:

Running Walk — This is the signature gait of the Tennessee Walking Horse and is a basic, loose, four-cornered gait with each of the horse's hooves hitting the ground separately at regular intervals. The sequence is left front, right rear, right front, and left rear. As the Walking Horse moves, its head will nod in rhythm with the regular rise and fall of its hooves.

Fox Trot — This is a gait that is also associated with a specific breed: the Missouri Fox Trotter. It is basically a diagonal gait like the trot, but the horse appears to walk with its front legs and trot with the rear. Because of the sliding action of the rear feet, rather than the harder step and suspension of a normal trot, the rider experiences little jarring action and can easily sit the gait. This, of course, also means there is less concussion on the horse's limbs than is the case with the trot.

Pacing — Many Standardbreds race at the trot. But some are bred to pace. At this gait, left front and left rear and right front and right rear move in unison, with the body rolling from side to side to remain in balance. It is something of a man-made gait, but certain individuals representing certain bloodlines will pace naturally.

The pace.

Amble — A pace at walking speed; however, the hind foot lands just before the front foot on the same side, with no period of suspension, such as at the trot.

Rack — This is a gait similar to the running walk, except that there is little or no overreach and the horse's head does not nod.

Singlefoot, Broken Amble — Both describe an exaggerated walk that resembles a pace. In this case, the hind foot strikes the ground an instant before the front foot on the same side.

Three-Gaited — This term normally is used with American Saddlebreds in the show ring. The horse travels at an animated walk, high-stepping trot, and animated canter.

Five-Gaited — The term is applied primarily to show ring Saddlebreds. Here the horse travels at the walk, animated trot, slow gait (like the rack only slower), canter, and rack.

WALKING IS EASY

The walk is the gait of choice for most horses. A band of wild horses traveling from grazing area to water hole or from one meadow of grass to another will almost always do so at the walk. The only time they break into a run is when they are startled or are fleeing from a real or imagined predator.

It is the same with domesticated horses which roam in a pasture or paddock. Unless they are brimming with energy after being confined or are anxious to join companions at the far end of the pasture, horses will walk.

There are many variations of the walk. Some horses mince along with tiny steps and short stride while others travel freely, giving you the feeling that shoulder and leg joints are operating on well-oiled ball bearings.

If you are looking for a trail riding horse, you should be looking for the animal with a long, fluid stride at the walk; one that can cover ground smoothly and rapidly while providing the person aboard with a comfortable ride. If, however, you are looking for a Tennessee Walking Horse to show, the definition of walk might be totally different. Because of the manner in which they are trained and shod, these horses take high-reaching steps in front, with an over-reaching action in the rear. This doesn't mean that Tennessee Walking Horses can't do a normal, flat-footed walk; it merely means that the walk in the show ring is different than the walk down a country lane.

The four-beat walk puts little stress on the legs. If all a horse had to do was walk, it could survive quite well even with conformational faults. However, that has never been the case. In the wild, nature culled in cruel fashion. Horses which could not run from predators were killed and eaten. The result was a gene pool of horses with strong, sturdy legs and hard hooves. The demand that horses travel at gaits faster and more animated than the walk continues today. But man has not done a good job of culling based on leg conformation.

THE TROT TELLS

The trot is the gait at which many conformational faults surface. The following terms describe some of these problems:

Interfering — This is the term used when a horse accidentally strikes its leg anywhere between the coronary band and the cannon bone with the opposite foot. Such problems can occur with front and rear legs.

Forging — This problem occurs when the toe of the hind foot hits the heel area of the forefoot on the same side.

Overreaching — The toe of the hind foot catches the forefoot on the same side, usually striking the heel. It is like forging, only more exaggerated.

Brushing — A general term for light striking, such as in forging and interfering.

Cross Firing — This is a problem that most frequently surfaces with pacing horses, with the inside of the hind foot hitting the inside quarter of the diagonal forefoot.

Elbow Hitting — This is a problem that usually surfaces only with horses carrying weighted shoes. It involves striking the elbow with the shoe of the same limb.

Scalping — The toe of the forefoot hits the coronary band or above on the rear foot of the same side. It may also strike the front of the cannon bone or pastern.

Speedy Cutting — Any type of limb interference at a fast gait.

While most contact problems are the result of poor conformation, they can occur in well-conformed horses engaged in fast and strenuous activity, such as barrel racing or cutting, where weight is suddenly shifted and the horse is off balance. No matter what the gait, a horse's ability to move forward in sustained fashion and remain sound requires good conformation. Next, a look at front leg conformation.

CHAPTER 2

Front Leg Conformation

When the subject of conformation is being discussed, the architectural term relating "form to function" is frequently heard. It was first applied to equine conformation by Professor Byron Good of Michigan State University. Conformation, he said, demonstrates the "relationship of form to function."

Obviously, he did not say that every horse is, or should be, constructed in exactly the same way. Quite the opposite is true. The best "form to function" is vastly different if you are looking for a nimble cutting horse, a racehorse that could run a mile rapidly, or an endurance horse that could travel 50 to 100 miles in a day and still remain sound.

The front legs bear more weight.

The legs of a good cutting horse should be short and muscular. This horse should have a sloping croup to enable it to slide to a stop and, in the blink of an eye, propel its body in a new direction, all at top speed. A racehorse able to perform effectively at the distance of a mile or more would be taller, longer, and leaner with more leg and perhaps a more level topline.

While horsemen might take some latitude in describing the optimum "form to function," depending on their discipline, there should be little latitude or compromise in defining good conformation, whether we are talking about a little cutting horse, a racehorse, a 17-hand jumper, or a horse used for dressage.

No matter what the "form to function," the horse must have good legs and feet. Think of the legs and feet as you would the foundation of a house. If a house's foundation is faulty, eventually

> ## AT A GLANCE
>
> - The forelegs support up to 65% of a horse's weight.
>
> - Proper alignment of the bones of the foreleg is the key to good conformation.
>
> - The better the conformation of the forelegs, the more likely a horse will remain sound.
>
> - The angles of the bones in the forelegs determine the quality of the horse's stride. The straighter the angles, the choppier the stride.
>
> - The angles of those bones determine how well a horse absorbs concussion while moving.

the house will crumble, no matter how pretty or stately it might appear. The same principle applies with horses. The feet and legs of a horse are its foundation. If the legs and feet aren't strong and durable, they will not hold up, no matter how handsome or athletic that horse might appear to be. The old adage, "…no feet, no horse" also applies to the legs. "No legs, no horse."

The conformation of a horse's front legs and feet requires particularly close examination and evaluation. That's because a horse carries between 60% to 65% of its weight on its front legs. At all gaits and even while standing, this uneven weight distribution brings additional stress to bear on the horse's front legs.

Before going any further, let's establish one basic premise: the horses described here will be used for competition or pleasure riding. Obviously, if a horse has conformational faults of the limbs, but has nothing to do all day but roam a pasture or stand in a box stall, its problems might not compromise its ability merely to exist. If, on the other hand, the horse is used on a regular basis, its conformational faults matter.

Although certain things about a horse can be changed or improved — health and physical fitness, for example — conformation cannot. Corrective shoeing might help somewhat and devices can be applied to a young horse in an effort to straighten misshapen legs, but that is about it. If the horse's problem is inherited, corrective trimming or shoeing does nothing to change its poor genetic makeup. If a horse with inherited faults winds up in a breeding program, its offspring stand a good chance of suffering from the same problems.

Therefore, picking a horse with good conformation becomes imperative if you want a horse that will perform well, remain sound, and be able to pass on its good traits if placed in a breeding band.

There are, of course, exceptions to every rule. Some horses can perform admirably despite conformation flaws. Racing and other disciplines are filled with examples of horses which overcome defects to excel in their fields.

STRUCTURE OF THE FORELEG

Let's take a close look at a horse's front legs. Interestingly, the bones of a horse's front legs are not connected to its skeleton. The entire front leg, from scapula on down, could be amputated without the scalpel ever touching bone. The horse's front legs are connected to its skeleton by a network of muscles, ligaments, and tendons. In a manner of speaking, the front legs form a sling that supports the forward part of a horse's body.

To examine the front end of a horse from the shoulders on down, a key word at this juncture is angle. Not only do the horse's front limbs support as much as 65% of its weight, they must serve as a shock absorber system that reduces the concussion of each step, whether walking, running, jumping, or stopping abruptly. If all of the bones, tendons, and ligaments existed in a perfectly straight line from bottom to top, the concussion from each step would travel from ground to shoulder without being absorbed. If, however, there is appropriate angle of foot, fetlock, and shoulder, much of the concussion will be dissipated along the way.

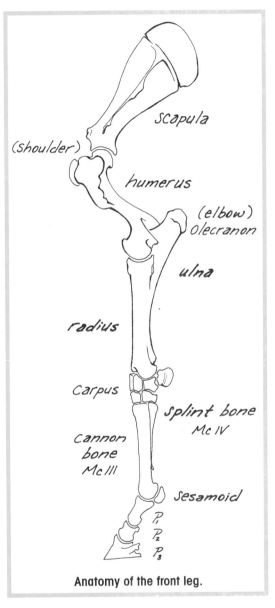

Anatomy of the front leg.

A horse with good conformation will have a front shoulder that is laid back or angled at an appropriate degree. Just exactly what that degree is will vary from horse to horse. The angle is key to the horse's stride. If the shoulder is very steep, the horse's stride will be short and choppy, which is always uncomfortable for the rider. The horse's front feet will hit the ground more often over a given distance, with the concussion from each step traveling all the way up the leg and into the body.

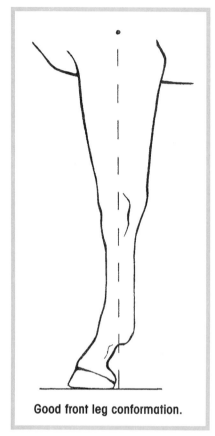

Good front leg conformation.

Next, look at the horse's shoulder bone or scapula. It is a broad bone that connects to the humerus. The humerus angles down and rearward and joins the radius or forearm at the elbow. The radius extends downward to the knee or carpus. Connecting to the bottom part of the carpus is the metacarpus or cannon bone, which runs down into the pastern. The long pastern bone is known as the first phalanx or P1. It fits into the second phalanx or P2, also known as the short pastern bone. The second phalanx fits into the third phalanx or P3, more commonly known as the coffin bone.

Just behind the cannon bone, where it joins the long pastern bone, are the sesamoid bones, which serve as pulleys for the deep flexor tendons. Another bone of the foot which is heavily involved with the suspensory ligaments is the distal sesamoid bone, located at the junction of the short pastern bone and the coffin bone. Most of us call it the navicular bone.

There are two other important bones in each of the front

legs. They travel down from the knee on either side of the cannon bone and are known as splint bones. They really don't serve much purpose. It is believed they are evolutionary remnants from the prehistoric three-toed horse. Though they might serve little practical purpose today, they can be involved in lameness problems.

When a horse is viewed in profile, one with good conformation will appear to have a straight, vertical alignment from the middle of its forearm all the way to the ground just behind its heel. Textbooks on good conformation often include a photograph of a horse in profile with a vertical line superimposed on the horse's forearm.

When looking at the horse from the front, superimpose a vertical line and it should travel in a straight path from the point of the shoulder, through the middle of the forearm, and down the cannon bone, pastern, and foot.

From the side, look for the angle formed by the ground under the hoof and the slope of the pastern. As is the case with the shoulder, this angle will vary from horse to horse.

Often a horse will have about the same degree of angle to its

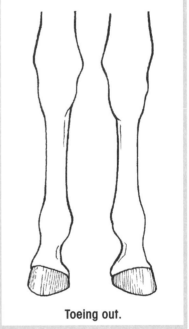

Toeing out.

pastern as it does in its shoulder. At one time, horsemen claimed that horses with the best conformation had front pasterns at a 45-degree angle to the ground. That claim is no longer considered valid. There is no universal degree for all horses. Today, 45 degrees would be considered the minimum

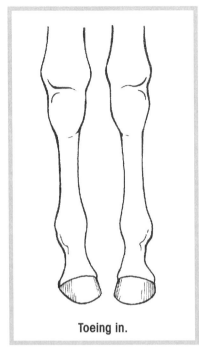

Toeing in.

acceptable angle in front for most horses.

One thing is critical: the slope of the pastern should be identical to the slope of the foot. If identical, there will be a precise and smooth insertion of the long pastern bone into the short pastern bone and of the short pastern bone into the coffin bone. If these bones do not mesh correctly, strain is placed on tendons and ligaments and lameness often results.

A horse with properly conformed legs can be evaluated according to this formula: the distance between its limbs at its chest will be the same as the distance between its feet on the ground. If the distance is narrower at the feet, the horse is base-narrow; if the reverse is true, it is base-wide.

CONFORMATIONAL FAULTS VIEWED FROM THE FRONT

Few horses have ideal conformation. A great many do not have good conformation. Many will deviate in one way or another from the ideal. How much deviation is involved will generally determine whether the horse can perform and still remain sound.

One of the most serious front leg conformational defects is toeing out. A horse with this fault is going to put extra stress on the inside of its knee with every stride. There is another problem, as wellAs the horse travels, particularly at the trot, it will wing in. This poses a constant danger to the horse of striking the sesamoids, the splint bones, and coronet band of its opposite leg. Frequently, the pressure transmitted to the inside of the front legs also will result in splints, those bony spurs on the inside of the front legs.

The reverse problem occurs in a horse that toes in or is pigeon-toed. Such a horse will have a tendency to paddle when it moves, but at least isn't in danger of striking itself.

A fault that is about as bad as the severely toed-out horse is one that is referred to as being bench-kneed. This means that the forearm and cannon bone do not line up. The forearm will enter the knee on the inside or medial aspect while the cannon bone will exit more on the outside or lateral aspect of the knee. Such a horse is likely to develop knee trouble when asked to perform in a stressful discipline.

Looking at the bones in a horse's knee, it is a wonder that it can stand up to stress, even when its conformation is nearly perfect. The bones in the knee remind me of a child's building blocks. With that illustration in mind, it becomes easy to understand why deviations from normal conformation, such as bench-knees, can create serious soundness problems. Unless one bone blends smoothly into another at the joints, the effects of weight and concussion are not properly handled.

There are other variations that can compromise a horse's ability to perform effectively and remain sound. Some of them combine a number of defects. Here are several examples:

Plaiting — Some horses that are base-narrow and toe out tend to place one forefoot directly in front of another. The horseman's phrase about "...a horse that can walk in a bicycle track" applies here. This structural fault can produce interference and stumbling when an advancing forelimb hits one that has been placed in front of it.

Base-Narrow, Toe In — This defect causes excessive strain on the ligaments of the fetlock and pastern joints. Windpuffs, ringbone, and sidebone often result.

Base-Narrow, Toe Out — This double fault adds another dimension to the problem when a narrow-based horse toes out and worsens its condition because great strain is placed on the limbs below its fetlocks.

Base-Wide, Toe Out — This condition also places great strain on the ligaments at the fetlock and pastern joints.

Base-Wide, Toe In — This is not a common fault, but it does occur. As the horse with this defect travels, it places undue strain on the inside of its front limbs.

The key to checking front leg conformation is to observe the horse in motion as well as at rest. Corrective shoeing or trimming might diminish the appearance of some conformational defects, but man-made solutions to poor conformation cannot change the bone structure that caused the problem in the first place. The problem horse whose hooves have been modified to cover up a toeing-in or -out problem might look straight and correct when standing, but its problem will surface at the trot, sometimes in bold fashion.

The only way a horse has a chance of remaining sound is to trim or shoe the foot to the direction or angle nature dictated. The defect will remain, but at least the horse has the advantage of the existing muscle, tendon, and ligament structure being aligned in a way that provides the most strength and durability.

CONFORMATIONAL FAULTS VIEWED FROM THE SIDE

Now for a critical look at the front limbs from the side view. Perhaps the worst conformation fault from this perspective is a horse that is behind at the knee or calf-kneed. A leg that is calf-kneed is a limb that can put a lot of stress on ligaments and tendons and, of course, on the knee joint. A horse with this kind of conformation fault probably would not remain sound if used as a jumper. Nor is it a desirable trait in a racehorse. This conformational fault often results in bone chips in the knee joint when the horse has been asked to run at speed.

The opposite problem, being over at the knee, or buck-kneed, is also a conformation fault, but one that is not as severe as being calf-kneed. At least the knee is made to bend in that direction. However, it is a problem that puts stress on joints, ligaments, and tendons.

There are a number of other variations from the norm that might be viewed from the side angle. They include:

Tied-In Knees — In such cases, the flexor tendons appear

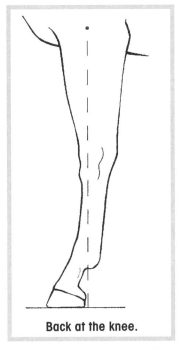

Back at the knee.

to be too close to the cannon bone just below the knee. This condition inhibits free movement.

Standing Under — This is a deviation in which the entire forelimb from the elbow down is placed back from the perpendicular and too far under the body. This condition causes excessive wear and fatigue of bones, ligaments, and tendons.

Camped In Front — This condition is just the opposite of the above, with the forelimb from the body to the ground being too far forward. Horses with this fault are prone to navicular disease as well as numerous other problems.

Short Upright Pasterns — Short, straight pasterns do little to dissipate concussion when a horse moves. Horses with this problem are more apt to develop navicular disease, ringbone, and arthritis.

Long Sloping Pasterns — This conformation fault also is referred to as being coon-footed. The pastern slope will probably be under 45 degrees. Occasionally, the pasterns are so weak that the fetlocks strike the ground.

Long Upright Pasterns — The problems associated with this conformation fault are about the same as with the short, upright pasterns, however, the horse's problems are more acute because concussion is increased. Traumatic arthritis and navicular disease often result from this fault.

If you are examining a horse in the presence of an oldtime horseman, he might tell you that you should be looking for "flat bone" when examining the cannon bone. Technically, there is no such thing as a flat bone in a horse's leg. The bones are round. What the horseman really is saying is that you should be looking for a sound-looking leg containing a large, round bone with correspondingly large tendons and ligaments that, when viewed from the side, give the leg the appearance of being flat.

While the bones are key elements in a horse's limbs, they would be of no value without the muscle, tendon, and ligament structures that hold everything together and allow the legs to function by supporting weight and propelling the horse forward and backward.

A tendon is a tough cord or band of dense, white, fibrous connective tissue that unites a muscle with bone and transmits the force which the muscle exerts. Key tendons are the deep digital flexor and the superficial digital flexor tendons. Both originate at the humerus and travel downward. The superficial flexor tendon connects to both the long and the short pastern bones. The deep digital flexor tendon connects to the coffin bone. These tendons transmit force from muscles and play a key role in making it possible for a horse to lift its foot to take a step.

A ligament is an equally tough band of tissue that connects the articular extremities of bone. Ligaments and tendons enable joints to function. The tendons and ligaments of the forelimbs can remain strong and function appropriately only when they are in proper alignment.

When you evaluate a horse's overall conformation, look for an animal that is balanced — one in which all the lines flow smoothly together. Properly conformed legs are just one part of that balanced picture. Each bone should flow smoothly into the joint where it connects with another bone, making for legs that are strong and durable. Now for a look at the rear legs.

CHAPTER 3

Rear Leg Conformation

Good conformation of a horse's rear legs is just as important as good conformation of its front legs. A horse unable to propel itself forward because of poorly constructed rear legs will not do for riding or driving.

The horse's front legs sustain more concussion at the lope or canter and gallop, but the rear legs, in addition to being the prime propelling force, also act as the horse's brakes. Just watch a reining or cutting horse in action. It can bring its rear legs forward and slide to a stop after traveling at a dead run. In a flash, a cutting horse also can roll back over its hocks to face the opposite direction and, just as quickly, use the driving power of its back legs to accelerate once again.

Trail horses traveling across mountainous terrain also need strong, durable rear legs that can propel them up steep slopes and slow the rate of descent when coming

A reining horse using its rear legs.

down. Jumpers, too, need strong, sound rear legs to launch their heavy bodies into the air. Upper-level dressage horses make great use of their rear legs as well.

To examine rear leg conformation, start at the spine where the ilium, the largest of three bones in the pelvis, connects with the spinal column. The angular shape of the horse's pelvis determines whether it has a flat croup or a sloped croup. More about that in a bit. The ilium angles down and rearward to blend into the femur or thigh bone. The femur

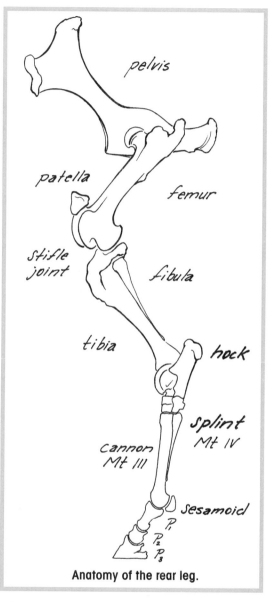

Anatomy of the rear leg.

angles slightly forward to the stifle. Beginning at the stifle is the tibia, which continues downward to the hock. From the hock to the pastern is the metatarsus or rear cannon bone, which flows downward into the long pastern bone, short

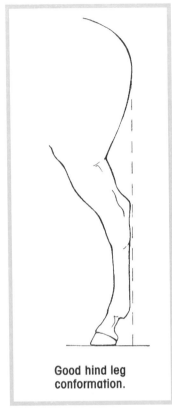

Good hind leg conformation.

pastern bone, and coffin bone.

The two key areas in the rear limbs where lameness often strikes are the hocks and stifles. The majority of lameness problems will occur in and around the hocks, with lameness of the stifle holding second place.

The stifle is the joint at which the femur ends and the tibia begins. Relating it to human anatomy, the stifle serves the same function as a human's knee. A horse's hocks play a key role because tendons pass over them to transmit energy from the muscles to provide propulsion. Unless the hock is properly conformed, each step produces undue stress. Lameness is frequently the result.

Let's start by examining a horse from the rear view to determine back leg conformation. Look for an evenly balanced horse, one with the distance between its thigh area and hocks being the same as the distance between its hind feet at ground level. The hind legs of a well-conformed horse should be straight. If a vertical line were drawn on a photo taken from behind, the line would go as straight as a plumb line from the center of the buttocks, downward through the center of the entire rear leg, including pastern and foot. This type of good conformation enables a horse to use its rear end to best advantage, while placing balanced stress on bones, muscles, tendons, and ligaments.

Now, assess the same parts of the horse from the side. When you look at the rear legs from this view, keep the term angulation, or the angular shape, in mind. The angle of the stifle and the hock should be neither too straight nor too angular, but should present a well-balanced picture, with muscles running smoothly down the leg to the hock.

Using an imaginary plumb line again, you should be able to start it at the rear of the buttocks and drop a straight line downward to the hock and then along the cannon bone until it reaches the ground three to four inches behind the heel.

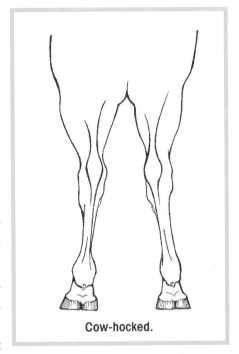

Cow-hocked.

As is the case with front limb conformation, many horses will have good rear limb conformation, while others will deviate from the ideal. The extent of deviation will determine how sound the horse remains when placed in disciplines that put heavy stress on the rear limbs.

The following list includes some conformation faults found in horses' hind legs:

Cow-hocked — A cow-hocked horse has hocks closer together than the distance between its hind feet. Typically a cow-hocked horse will be narrow at the hocks, and base-wide at the feet, often with its hooves turned out. Just how serious this conformation problem is depends upon the amount of deviation from the ideal. A mildly cow-hocked horse might be able to perform well in a number of disciplines. However, if the fault is severe, the horse will have problems with interfering. Severely cow-hocked horses also place heavy stress on

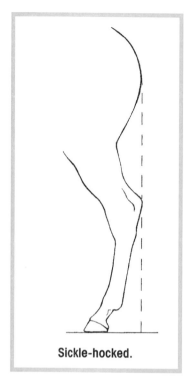

Sickle-hocked.

their hocks, especially the inside or medial aspect, and this can result in a condition known as bone spavin.

Base-Narrow — A base-narrow horse has a hock problem that is the reverse of the base-wide problem. In such cases, the base-narrow horse's feet are closer together than its hocks and thigh area. Undue stress is placed on the hocks with each stride which can quickly compromise soundness. In addition, the base-narrow horse will never be an outstanding athlete because it is unable to make proper use of muscle power either in propelling itself forward or putting on the brakes. Base-narrow conformation behind can cause interference problems plus other problems involving the hock.

Variations and Combinations — There are variations and combinations of conformation problems. For example, a horse might be base-narrow from the fetlocks down or might be both cow-hocked and sickle-hocked. Such conformation faults can be spotted when looking at the horse either at rest or when in motion.

Now, let's take a look at some conformation deviations when viewing the horse from the side:

Sickle-hocked — Looking at a perfectly conformed horse, you might imagine a plumb line that travels vertically down the rear of the cannon bone to the ground. When a horse is sickle-hocked, its cannon bone is forward from a vertical line. Again, the severity of the deviation often determines whether the horse can remain sound when being used. A severe deviation puts a great deal of stress on the rear of the hock and can quickly bring unsoundness. A mild deviation will still put extra stress on the rear of the hock, but might not compromise soundness to the same degree. Horses with sickle hocks are predisposed to curbs.

Straight Behind — This condition results when there is very little angulation between the thigh bone or femur and the tibia. This condition places heavy stress on the stifle joint as well as on the hock. If the horse is used for heavy work, such as roping, cutting, or reining, it will be prone to injury as a result of legs which are unable to make proper use of working muscles that are designed to dissipate concussion.

AT A GLANCE

- The rear legs serve as the horse's prime propelling force.

- The rear legs also serve as the brakes.

- Strong, durable rear legs are important in nearly every equine discipline.

- Good rear leg conformation is as important as good front leg conformation.

- Rear leg lameness often involves the stifles or the hocks.

Standing Under — In this condition, the horse's rear legs are placed too far forward. The same problems associated with a sickle-hocked horse would accompany this condition.

Camped Out — This condition is the reverse of standing under, with the horse's rear legs being located too far to the rear. A camped-out horse will not be able to get its hind legs under it for either propulsion or good braking.

Still looking at the rear limbs from the side view, check the horse's pasterns. The slope of the pastern should be the same as the slope of the foot so that the long pastern bone, short pastern bone, and coffin bone all fit smoothly and neatly together. Due to the greater angles of the rear legs, compared with the front, the rear pasterns normally will have a steeper slope — often in the 50- to 55-degree range.

Also from the side, observe the horse's croup. Here again we come to the issue of form to function. The shape of the croup,

This horse has a fairly flat croup.

corresponding to the way in which the pelvis is attached, determines to a large extent if the horse can translate the power generated by its rear legs into motion.

First, the way the croup is constructed determines a horse's length of stride. When propelling itself forward, a horse with a flat croup is not going to be able to reach far forward with its rear legs, but those legs are capable of extending far to the rear. This gives the horse with a flat croup a relatively long, flowing stride.

If its croup is sloped, a horse will be able to reach farther forward with its rear legs, but won't be able to extend them as far to the rear. This is the type of croup sought by riders of

A sloped croup is seen in this draft horse.

cutters, reining, and roping horses. Horses with sloping croups generally can reach far under themselves for good purchase and also are able to slam on the brakes for a hard stop when traveling at speed.

An exaggeration of a sloped croup is often seen in draft horses. Their croups can be very steep because they are designed to take only short, but powerful steps when propelling themselves forward while pulling a heavy load.

As with the front end, the angulation and length of bones in the animal's rear are extremely important. The thigh bone has to be long enough to reach the stifle and the tibia has to be of the proper length and angle to fit smoothly into the hock. The rear cannon bone should be short to help the tendons and ligaments over the hock exert proper pull.

Now for a closer look at joints and how poor conformation at those points can predispose a horse to lameness.

CHAPTER 4

The Joints

Joints are the structures which enable one bone to move against another. They permit a horse to lift, flex, and bend its legs. Joints also absorb concussion while the horse is moving.

Sound joints allow a horse to function properly; unsound joints often result in lameness. Once again, conformation faults can cause many of the problems that affect joints. A horse with good conformation puts balanced stress on its joints when performing while the horse with poor conformation produces unbalanced stress that can create problems.

There are three types of equine joints: synovial, or movable; cartilaginous, or slightly movable; and fibrous, or immovable.

Synovial joints are the ones most apt to sustain injury or to be attacked by disease. In a manner of speaking, synovial joints are the horse's ball bearings. A synovial joint consists of two bone ends covered by articular cartilage. The cartilage within the joint is smooth and resilient, allowing for frictionless movement.

The other joint categories are immovable joints, which are found in the skull and between the shafts of long bones, and cartilaginous joints, such as the pelvis and vertebrae, which have limited movement. The growth plates which extend a bone's length during the animal's early, developing years are also cartilaginous joints.

Joint stability is maintained by a fibrous joint capsule, which attaches to both bones and collateral ligaments. The collateral ligaments are located on either side of most synovial joints. They are important mechanisms that maintain stability in joints such as the fetlocks, knees, elbows, hocks, and stifles. The cruciate ligaments also help to maintain stability within some joints, such as the stifle.

Other ligaments outside the joint cavity lend their support as well. Prime examples include the distal sesamoidean ligaments and suspensory ligaments that, together with the sesamoid bones, make up the suspensory apparatus and hold the fetlock in position.

AT A GLANCE

- Joints absorb concussion as the horse moves.

- Synovial joints, those which are movable, are the ones most prone to injury or disease.

- The knee is composed of three major joints.

- Most joint injuries occur in the front legs because of the weight load.

- The hind leg has two major joints: the stifle and the hock.

- Treating joint injuries can range from the use of cold water and ice to arthroscopic surgery, depending on the severity of the problem.

Each joint capsule also contains an inner lining called the synovial membrane. It secretes synovial fluid, which provides lubrication within the joint itself. As a result of its unique structure, a healthy joint has frictionless motion, provided by smooth articular cartilage and lubrication.

Hyaluronic acid is a normal component of joints and is an integral component of both synovial fluid and articular cartilage in normal joints. It acts as a cementing substance attaching the joints' structures. When joints become diseased, there is often a depletion of hyaluronic acid that compromises the joint's ability to function properly.

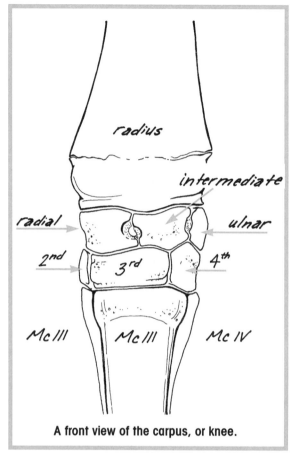

A front view of the carpus, or knee.

JOINT BY JOINT

Let's take a look at some individual joints, beginning with the front limbs. Injuries to joints of the front limbs are more numerous than those in the rear because of the heavier weight bearing down on front legs and the concussive factors involved when a horse runs at speed or jumps. While the mechanical engineering of most joints is basically excellent, there are exceptions, notably the knee, or carpal joint.

A horse's knee is composed of three main joints, two of which are in actual use, and numerous ligaments which keep everything tied into place. This is a Herculean task because a horse's knee contains eight individual bones.

While they look a bit like building blocks gone awry, the bones of the knee are arranged into two neat rows. Included in the top row are the radial carpal bone, intermediate carpal bone, ulnar carpal bone, and accessory carpal bone. In the bottom row are the first (when present), second, third, and fourth carpal bones. This structure rests on top of the cannon bone, which is flanked on either side by splint bones. Resting on top of this carpal, or knee structure, is another bone, the radius.

When one considers the intricate nature of the carpal structure, the benefits of good conformation become even more important. Horses with poor leg conformation, such as those which are calf-kneed, bench-kneed, or buck-kneed, are going to place unbalanced stress on this complicated joint, and injuries or diseases often result.

This racehorse's pastern is almost parallel to the ground.

Below the knee, the cannon bone continues, then joins with the long pastern bone or P1 at the fetlock joint. Also located at this junction are the medial and lateral proximal sesamoid bones. Although the proximal sesamoid bones are deeply embedded in, and supported by, the suspensory ligament, they are subject to fracture because of concussion or injury when a horse interferes and strikes them with the opposing limb.

When a racehorse runs at top speed, there is one point in every stride where its entire weight descends upon one front leg, with most of the concussion being absorbed and dissipated by the fetlock joint. Take a look at a photo of a racehorse coming down the home stretch when all of the weight and concussion passes to that leading foreleg. Its pastern will be almost parallel to the ground. The change in angle from approximately 50 degrees when at rest to being almost level at nearly zero degrees demonstrates how extremely strong and flexible the fetlock joint must be.

The next joint below the fetlock is called the pastern joint, which is the place where the long pastern bone, P1, connects with the short pastern bone, P2. The pastern joint is the least movable of all of the joints from the fetlock to the foot and absorbs only a minimum of concussion.

A horse's foot has joints, too. The coffin joint is composed of the short pastern bone, P2, the coffin bone, P3, and the navicular bone. The coffin joint has a great deal of elasticity and works as an effective shock absorber. An intricate process occurs within the coffin joint with each stride as this network of bones and joints works to distribute concussion and weight.

The deep digital flexor tendon, which supports the navicular bone from behind and below, enables it to function in its weight-transferring and shock-absorbing capacity. The deep flexor tendon is closely fitted to the surface of the navicular bone with a navicular bursa, a fluid-filled sac, that provides a smooth lubricating substance that reduces friction.

Here again, good conformation helps the horse to remain sound. Conformation faults such as an overly steep pastern and foot, for example, make it impossible for the proper transfer of weight and concussion absorption within the coffin joint. Instead, undue pressure is brought to bear on the small navicular bone and injury or disease often result in serious lameness.

There are two other key joints in the forelegs: the shoulder joint and the elbow joint. However, because a good deal of concussion already has been absorbed by the time its effect reaches these two joints, they are less prone to injury.

The scapula, or shoulder joint, is a ball-and-socket joint held in place by a strong web of ligaments, muscles, and tendons. It's such a strong joint that dislocation seldom occurs in horses. Medial and lateral ligaments stabilize the elbow joint. It works like a hinge, with movement limited to one plane, or direction. Medial refers to the structures toward the inside of a horse's legs, while lateral refers to structures situated toward the outside.

The rear leg of a horse includes two additional joints of great importance: the hock joint and the stifle joint. The hock, or tarsal joint, is that spot where the long bone called the tibia is joined with the metatarsal bones. The hock joint is a bit like the front knee, or carpal joint, in that it is comprised of a number of bones. There are six bones in the hock joint, but they do not have the degree of motion found in the knee joint. Like the knee joint, however, the hock joint is held together by a complex set of ligaments which enable it to function. The bones of the hock joint include the calcaneus and talus on the top and the central tarsal bone, third tarsal bone, first, and second tarsal bones, which are fused, and the fourth tarsal bone. All of them rest on top of the metatarsal bones, cannon bone, and splint bones.

The second key joint of the rear limbs is the stifle joint, that spot where the tibia joins the femur. A horse's stifle corresponds to a human knee. It is the largest single joint in the horse's body. One function of the stifle joint is to cause the limb to become rigid when the foot is on the ground. This is done by contraction of muscles below the patella, a structure roughly equivalant to a human's knee cap.

Above the stifle joint is the hip joint, which is the clearest example of a ball-and-socket joint. It is stabilized by strong bands of ligaments. The head, or upper end, of the femur fits into the socket, or cavity, formed by the hip bone. One of the ligaments that stabilizes this joint, the accessory ligament, does not occur in any domestic animal other than the horse.

The fetlock, pastern, and coffin joints of the rear limbs correspond to their counterparts in the front legs. The prime differences are that they generally have a steeper angulation and are less subject to concussion because the rear end is used more for propulsion than weight bearing.

In each case, when discussing joints, we find that the joint's stability is facilitated by a complex network of tendons, ligaments, and muscles. When a horse has good conformation, such elements function in synchronized fashion to bear weight and absorb concussion. Conversely, poor conformation places unbalanced stress on these joints, often causing lameness problems.

There is a man-made problem that can occur in the joints of performing horses. Sometimes riders simply push their horses too much, forcing their joints to try to absorb concussion and stress beyond the range nature intended.

JOINT PROBLEMS

There are a number of conditions resulting from injuries in or around the joints that cause inflammation which, in turn, leads to the release of various enzymes and other agents that bring about joint deterioration. Such conditions include:

• Synovitis, which is an inflammation of the delicate synovial membranes.

• Capsulitis, which is an inflammation of the fibrous joint capsule. This condition usually is present with synovitis and vice versa.

•Articular cartilage and bone fragmentation or fracture.

• Tearing of ligaments.

• Osteoarthritis, which is the result of severe joint injuries and of injuries that are not treated adequately. Its symptoms include swelling and pain plus the progressive loss of articular cartilage on the surface of the bone, which is a permanent condition that ultimately will lame the horse.

Whenever there is trauma to a joint, inflammation occurs. Inflammation stimulates the release of damaging enzymes and other problem agents known as free radicals, prostaglandins, and cytokines. These destructive elements attack the basic components of articular cartilage and set in motion a degenerative process that can render a horse unsound if not treated. The most obvious sign when synovitis and capsulitis are present is a puffy joint due to the accumulation of fluid. Early and aggressive treatment of the condition is vital.

TREATING JOINT PROBLEMS

One of the simplest ways to reduce joint inflammation is the application of cold water and ice. Therapeutic ultrasound and lasers can be effective. So can non-steroidal anti-inflammatory drugs such as phenylbutazone, Banamine, Naproxen, mecofenamic acid, and aspirin. These drugs — with phenylbutazone being used most frequently — inhibit the prostaglandins which cause pain and can be responsible for significant articular cartilage damage.

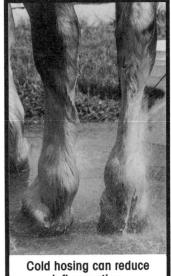

Cold hosing can reduce inflammation.

Another weapon in fighting joint disease is hyaluronic acid, which can be administered either directly into the joint or intravenously. Often, when a joint is injured, there is a depletion of hyaluronic acid and an injection might restore it to normal level. Another highly effective weapon is polysulfated glycosaminoglycan, commonly sold as Adequan. As with hyaluronic acid, glycosaminoglycans appear naturally in the joints and inhibit the effects of various enzymes associated with cartilage degeneration.

Corticosteroids are potent anti-inflammatory drugs that can

have immediate beneficial effects. But recent studies indicate that cortizone drugs might cause problems in joints that can make a horse unsound. However, several of the leading equine health-care researchers still maintain that corticosteroids can be both effective and safe for horses.

When a bone chip is discovered by a veterinarian, his or her most sucessful treatment is arthroscopic surgery. Whenever a chip fracture occurs, it involves the articular surface and the cartilage covering that surface. Bone debris can cause synovial inflammation. In many cases, when surgeons remove the bone chips or fragments arthroscopically, the horses recover and can be put back to work within a relatively short period of time.

There is a constant here, however, that can't be avoided. If the fracture or other joint problems have occurred as the result of poor conformation, there is always danger that the problems will resurface when the the horse's legs are placed under stress again. If poor conformation is involved and the stress is great enough, the horse could suffer a severe fracture within a

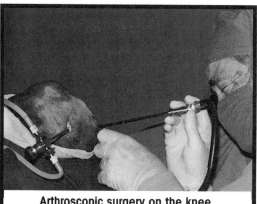

Arthroscopic surgery on the knee.

joint that will require far more extensive surgery than can be done arthroscopically. Fractures of this type can range from those that can be repaired surgically to those so severe that euthanasia is the only option.

While poor comformation is often the underlying cause of joint problems, horses with good conformation can suffer injuries and breakdowns due to excessive stress placed on their legs and fatigue suffered during strenuous competition or exercise. Yet one salient point remains true: a horse with good conformation will have far fewer problems than one with poor conformation. Next, a look at some of the specific maladies that can afflict a horse's legs.

CHAPTER 5
Specific Lameness Conditions

There are several reasons a horse can go lame. One is an external injury, such as a puncture wound to the foot, a wire cut, or a kick from another horse. Another is a stress injury resulting from some form of strenuous work. Poor conformation also can trigger lameness.

Subjecting a horse with poor conformation to strenuous activities can predispose it to stress injuries that might not affect a horse with better conformation. Leg and joint injuries due to poor conformation have been covered at length in previous chapters.

Many external injuries that cause lameness can be avoided through proper management procedures, such as providing the horse with an environment free of sharp objects and barbed wire fences.

Preventive measures get a little more complicated when dealing with the other two causes. There are lamenesses that are obvious and easy to diagnose, but there also are conditions in which a horse's ability to perform is compromised, but the cause is obscure and difficult to identify. Sometimes lameness results from a combination of problems, rather than a single cause. There also are lamenesses that can occur in the most well-conformed horses when the stress applied to that particular animal's bones, tendons, ligaments, and muscles is just simply more than can be borne.

The following list contains a mixture of terms veterinarians and horsemen use to describe the lamenesses that result from strenuous exercise or strenuous exercise combined with poor conformation:

• Arthritis is an inflammation of the joint. There are three forms of arthritis. Serous arthritis involves inflammation of the synovial membrane of a joint, usually as the result of trauma, and is accompanied by swelling. Infectious arthritis is what the term implies: an invasion of the joint by micro-organisms. Osteoarthritis is the final stage in a joint problem involving degenerative changes in bone and cartilage. It often comes in the wake of the other two forms of arthritis.

> ## AT A GLANCE
>
> • Lameness can stem from trauma, strenuous work, or poor management.
>
> • Poor conformation can contribute to future lameness problems such as curbs or bowed tendons.
>
> • Some lameness problems can be avoided or minimized with proper management and use of the horse.
>
> • Because of the weight load on their front legs, racehorses can develop bucked shins, splints, and other problems.
>
> • Fractures can range from minor to career-ending or fatal.

- Desmitis is an inflammation of a ligament.
- Osteitis is an inflammation in bone.
- Osteophytosis is the formation of an osteophyte, or bony growth.
- Periostitis is an inflammation of the periosteum, the sheath of tissue that covers bone.
- Synovitis is an inflammation of the synovial linings in such areas as the joint capsule and tendon sheath.
- Tendinitis is an inflammation of a tendon.
- Tenosynovitis is an inflammation of the synovial lining

OTHER CONDITIONS

Bucked Shins

Bucked shins normally occur in young racehorses when they begin training. It is inflammation of the periosteum, or sheath, covering the cannon bone and results from concussion. For years, horse trainers thought that the condition couldn't be avoided and simply had to be endured.

Recent research, much of it conducted at the University of Pennsylvania's New Bolton Center, indicates that a proper approach to the training of young horses can go a long way toward preventing bucked shins.

If the only problem associated with bucked shins were periostitis, it perhaps would be considered a minor malady. However, bucked shins often are coupled with microfractures that can lead to more serious fractures later in the horse's career.

When bucked shins do occur, the best remedy is rest and cold packs to relieve the inflammation. The inflammation usually makes the front of the shins sore and tender to the touch.

Bowed Tendon (Tendinitis)

This condition usually affects a horse performing at high speed, or racing. It almost always involves the superficial digital flexor tendon; sometimes it also involves the deep digital flexor tendon. Swelling and soreness along the tendons are symptoms. The "bow" will be classified as high, middle, or low, depending on its location.

Causes of tendinitis include over-extension, poor conditioning, poor conformation and fatigue, plus damage caused by poor racetrack conditions, improper trimming and shoeing (low heels, long toes), and inappropriate training techniques,

The veterinarian will get an overall impression of the horse (photo 1) before starting the lameness exam; the vet examines specific locations in the foreleg (photos 2 and 3).

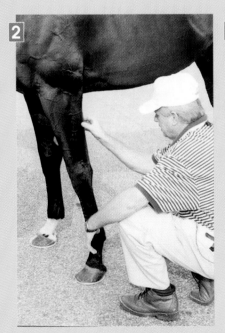

The veterinarian feels for a pulse (photo 4), which could indicate a problem; examining the tendons in the foreleg (photo 5); examining the pastern (photo 6).

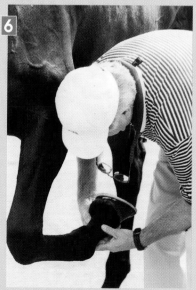

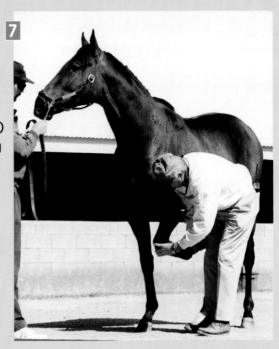

Palpating the knee (photo 7) can reveal soreness; flexing the knee (photo 8) and the ankle joint (photo 9) can produce a pain response if the horse is lame.

The veterinarian flexes the hock (photo 10) to determine if the horse is sore in that area; palpating the inside of the hock (photo 11), and seeking a pain response by further flexion (photo 12).

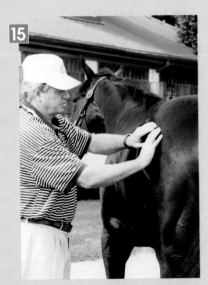

In photos 13-15, the veterinarian examines key muscles in the back and hip area, sometimes the source of lameness problems; in photo 16, checking the tautness of the tail can indicate the possibility of neurological disease or vertebral problems.

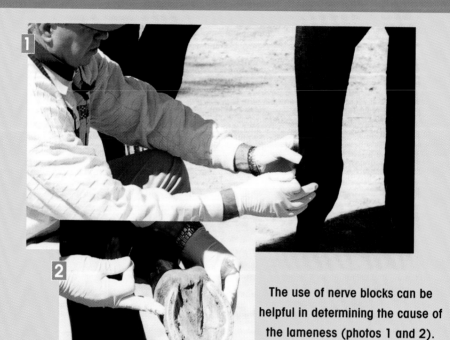

The use of nerve blocks can be helpful in determining the cause of the lameness (photos 1 and 2).

After narrowing down the problem area, the veterinarian can further the diagnosis with the use of radiographs (photos 3 and 4).

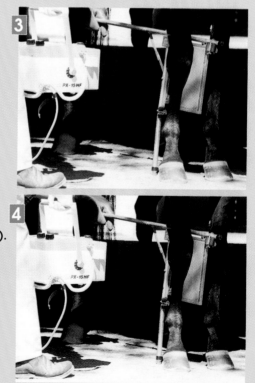

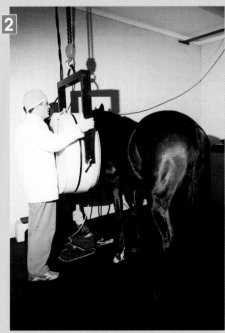

Treadmills (photos 1 and 3) can be used as a diagnostic aid in determining lameness, as can scintigraphy (photo 2).

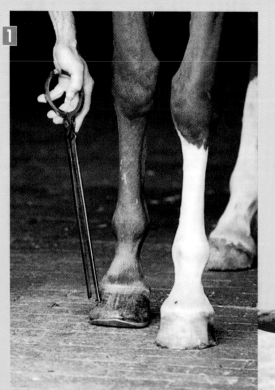

Laminitis, or founder, can cause pronounced changes in the appearance of the affected hoof (photo 1).

In severe cases, the hoof wall will slough off and a new exterior will grow (photo 2).

such as working a horse that already has some inflamed tendons.

During the acute stage, the horse is severely lame. There is both heat and swelling in the affected area as a result of the rupturing of tendon fibers, which brings about hemorrhage and edema.

Chronic cases develop fibrosis, the formation of fibrous tissue and adhesions in the damaged area. A horse with chronic tendinitis might appear sound while walking or trotting,

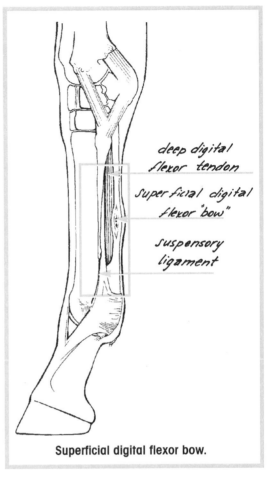

deep digital
flexor tendon

superficial digital
flexor "bow"

suspensory
ligament

Superficial digital flexor bow.

but becomes lame when it gallops.

It is best to treat a bowed tendon, or tendinitis, in the early, acute stage. Rest, plus treatment of inflammation with cold packs and anti-inflammatory drugs, is most important at this stage.

How well the tendon heals often depends on the severity of the "bow." Whatever the degree of injury, the horse should receive a long period of rest, then it should be brought back into training slowly and carefully.

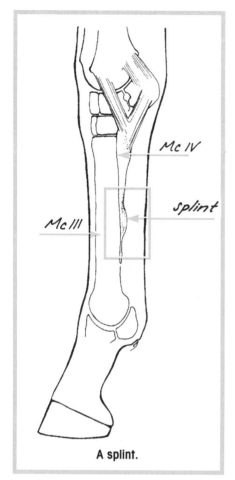

Mc IV

Splint

Mc III

A splint.

Splints

"Popping a splint" is a condition known as interosseous desmitis. While the condition ultimately results in a bony growth, the problem originates in the interosseous ligament between the splint bone and the cannon bone. It can occur in either the front legs or rear legs, but is much more common in the forelegs.

A number of factors can cause splints, including poor conformation. Some horses which toe out will wing in and strike themselves, resulting in injury. Trauma from concussion, strain from excessive training, and poor shoeing also can cause splints.

In reality, the condition is a periostitis that results in the production of new bone. Just how compromising a splint will be depends on its location. Unless its location hinders the action of an adjacent ligament, a splint will not cause long-term lameness. However, lameness is likely at the onset when splints are forming and will be most noticeable following exercise. The condition calls for complete rest until the soreness disappears.

Curb

This condition involves a thickening of the long plantar ligament that runs down the rear leg from hock to pastern.

Again, poor confor-
mation can be a
cause, along with
slipping, jumping,
and pulling. A curb
usually is located just
below the point of
the hock and is man-
ifested as an enlarge-
ment best observed
when looking at the
leg from the side. In
the acute stage, the
horse will be in pain
and will stand with
its heel elevated to
alleviate pressure on
the afflicted area.
The horse might not
be lame once the
initial inflammation
subsides. In the
acute stage, basic

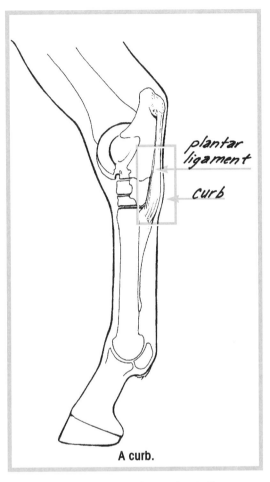

plantar ligament

curb

A curb.

treatment involves rest, plus cold packs to relieve the inflammation.

Bog Spavin

Bog spavin is technically known as tarsal hydrarthrosis and
is a chronic synovitis, or inflammation of the synovial lining,
within the hock joint. Poor conformation is often a culprit in
this condition; the horse that is too straight in the hock joint is
predisposed to bog spavin. Trauma also can be involved as a
result of quick stops, quick turning, as well as injury to the

hock joint. Whatever the cause, bog spavin is a distention, or swelling, of the joint capsule of the hock. This distention stimulates an excessive production of synovial fluid. Although unsightly, the condition does not always result in lameness.

Bone Spavin

This serious condition most frequently surfaces in horses with poor conformation. Both sickle-hocks and cow-hocks predispose a horse to bone spavin because they tend to impose a lot of stress on the front or medial aspect of the hock joint. Bone spavin is a bony enlargement of the hock joint due to osteoarthritis. An afflicted horse will tend to drag the toe on the affected limb, shortening the forward flight of the foot. When standing, a horse with bone spavin often rests its toe on the ground with its heel slightly raised. One diagnostic method involves flexing the hock joint for a minute or more, releasing it, then making the animal trot out. An afflicted horse generally will show pronounced lameness at the trot during such a test.

Horses with mild cases of bone spavin often will start out lame when being exercised, but as they warm up, their pain will diminish and they won't show signs of lameness. In severe cases, the opposite might be true — exercise will aggravate their lameness.

The ability of a horse to perform is compromised by bone spavin. There are surgical procedures that can alleviate bone spavin. Corrective shoeing can help relieve the pain.

Thoroughpin

Thoroughpin is tenosynovitis, or inflammation of the tarsal sheath. The distention of the tarsal sheath of the deep digital flexor tendon occurs just above the hock. It will be manifested as swelling in an area at the same level as the point of the hock. As such, it is sometimes confused with bog spavin. However, the swelling that results from thoroughpin is a few inches higher than that noted with bog spavin.

Thoroughpin is more of a blemish than a serious lameness problem. Treatment often involves withdrawal of fluid and injection of hyaluronic acid or, in some cases, a corticosteroid.

Ringbone

Ringbone is new bone growth that occurs on the surfaces of the long and short pastern bones and the coffin bone. It usually results in lameness. It stems from periostitis and can lead to osteoarthritis and ankylosis, defined as the crippling immobility and consolidation of a joint due to disease or injury.

Ringbone is characterized as being either high or low. High ringbone is new bone growth at the bottom (distal) end of the long pastern bone or top (proximal) end of the short pastern bone. Low ringbone is new growth at the distal end of the short pastern bone or the proximal end of the coffin bone.

Ringbone can occur in either the front or hind feet, but is more common in the front.

Poor conformation and trauma are usually the causative agents of ringbone. Horses which are base narrow and toe in or out are predisposed to ringbone toward the outsides of the legs, while horses which are base wide and toe

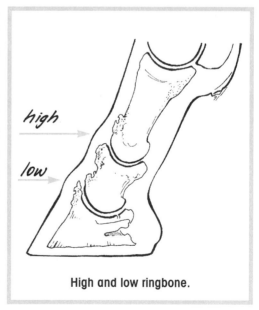

High and low ringbone.

in or out may be afflicted on the part of the joints toward insides of the legs due to the extra stress faulty conformation puts on the joints. Steep pasterns also predispose a horse to ringbone.

When ringbone occurs, there is a characteristic bell-shaped appearance to that part of the pastern. There will be lameness at the onset of the problem, but it might fade unless the joint surfaces themselves are involved. If the joint surfaces are involved, the prognosis is not good.

Complete rest at the onset is prescribed. In some cases, surgical procedures can be beneficial.

Quittor

Quittor is an extremely rare condition that results from trauma, such as injury to the coronary band through bruising or as the result of a wire cut. Quittor sometimes affects horses that interfere when they travel. Quittor also can result from a puncture wound to the sole. The front limbs are the ones normally affected. During the acute stage, lameness generally occurs.

The result of such an injury is a chronic inflammation of a collateral cartilage of the coffin bone or third phalanx. It is characterized by necrosis, or cell death, of the cartilage and a constant weeping, or drainage of pus through the coronary band.

Surgery can be used to remove diseased tissue and cartilage. However, if the damage is extensive and the coffin joint has been invaded, the prognosis for recovery is poor.

Corns and Bruises

A horse can bruise the sole of its foot which, in turn, can bring on lameness. Improper shoeing is frequently the cause of a form of bruise called a corn. The sensitive and insensitive tissues of the sole form a protective buttress that angles between the wall and the bar of the foot. Pressure from improper shoeing can bruise this tissue. Corns usually occur in the front feet.

There are three types of corns. Dry corns are the result of bruising of sensitive tissues and leave a red stain. Moist corns are the result of severe injury that results in the exudation of a moist serum from the injured sole. Suppurating corns are those that have become infected, resulting in the death of cells of the sensitive laminae.

The best treatment for corns, as well as the best preventive measure, is proper shoeing. Corns often are the result of improper shoeing or when shoes are left on the feet too long, bringing pressure to bear at the angle between wall and bar. Horses left barefoot rarely develop corns. Overreaching also might cause corns to develop.

Osselet

This problem occurs at the fetlock joint, causing calcification resulting from stretching and tearing of the joint capsule at the top, bottom, or both. Basically, it is traumatic arthritis of the fetlock.

Concussion is believed to be the main cause of osselets. Horses with upright pasterns are predisposed to the condition. It frequently shows up in young horses being trained for racing.

A horse with osselets has a short, choppy gait in the acute stage. Flexion of the fetlock joint will produce pain. If heavy exercise is continued, the horse will become progressively more lame.

During this inflammatory stage, the first treatment protocol is rest and the application of cold packs. Anti-inflammatory agents such as phenylbutazone often are administered.

Horses afflicted with osselets often recover and can return to competition. However, if the afflicted horse has steep pasterns, the prognosis is poor because there will be continued concussion at the fetlock joints, which are not designed to absorb and dissipate it.

Stringhalt

This is something of a mystery affliction that is quite uncommon today. No one is sure just what causes it. It occurs in rear limbs. Stringhalt is an involuntary flexion of the hock when the horse is in motion. It can vary from a very mild flexion while walking to a pronounced lifting of the foot toward the abdomen. Some horses will demonstrate excessive flexion with each step, while with others it is spasmodic.

Horses can be treated surgically for the condition by removing a portion of the tendon that crosses the lateral surface of the hock joint. Most horses will show improvement after surgery, but the degree of improvement varies.

Sesamoiditis

This is an inflammation of the proximal sesamoid bones. The ligaments that are involved with these bones also might be affected. The condition often shows up in racehorses, hunters, and jumpers, all of which place great stress on their fetlocks during competition.

The first order of treatment is rest and a reduction of the inflammation. The prognosis is guarded, depending on how much new bone growth has been stimulated on the sesamoid bones.

Windpuffs

This condition usually does not result in lameness, but it can be a warning sign that something is amiss. Windpuffs are fluid-filled swellings in the back of the fetlock joints in front or rear limbs. They usually are found in young horses in training.

Unless the horse goes lame, treatment is unnecessary. Windpuffs usually disappear spontaneously as the horse matures and becomes fitter. Interestingly, windpuffs once again can appear in older horses but seldom cause a problem.

Bursitis

Just as the name indicates, bursitis is an inflammation of the bursa. A bursa is a sac of fluid located within joints to prevent damage from friction.

Bursitis is often the result of trauma. The condition can show up in the shoulder, stifle, hock, hip, elbow, withers (fistulous withers), the knee, the navicular area, and the poll (poll evil). The condition can vary from a very mild synovitis to suppurative bursitis with the formation of an abscess.

Treatment involves reduction of the irritation within the bursa. Rest often is advocated. Aspiration of fluids (the removal of fluid through a hypodermic needle) and injection of corticosteroids are effective treatment protocols. In chronic cases, surgical removal of the bursa is done when the synovitis has become a persistent condition.

Hoof Cracks

These are cracks that either originate at the bottom of the foot and travel upward or begin at the coronary band as the result of trauma and run downward. The cracks are labeled as toe cracks, heel cracks, or quarter cracks, depending on location.

Lack of a proper trimming program often is implicated in hoof cracks. In most cases, frequent trimming and shoeing can resolve the problem, unless the crack is so deep that an infection has set in. The problem is more serious if it originates at the coronary band where hoof growth begins.

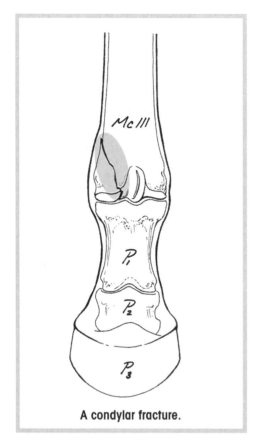

A condylar fracture.

Gravel

This is a term used to describe an infectious condition involving the white line between the hard, horny outer wall of the hoof and the sensitive inner surface of the foot. For years, horsemen thought that the condition resulted from a tiny piece of gravel migrating from the white line to the heel area.

In reality, a crack in the white line permits infection to invade the sensitive structures of the foot. There has to be drainage somewhere during the inflammatory process and the path it usually follows is to the heel area.

Treatment involves ensuring proper drainage and taking steps such as wrapping and packing the foot to prevent an invasion by harmful bacteria.

Thrush

This is a condition of the frog that results from keeping a horse in a dirty stall. The condition is easy to see — and smell! The horse's frog will yield a black discharge that has a putrid odor.

Maintaining a horse in clean, dry surroundings and cleaning its feet regularly are the best deterrents and also serve as the most appropriate treatment. An anti-bacterial medication, such as Coppertox, along with daily hoof cleaning and clean surroundings, usually clears up the problem quickly.

Fractures

Fractures can range from a minor problem, such as a bone chip that can be removed arthroscopically, to a catastrophic accident, when a bone shatters and the only option is euthanasia.

Any fracture will cause lameness and must be dealt with immediately. Surgical techniques have improved greatly in recent years. Only a few years ago, horses were routinely put down whenever fractures were detected. Modern, life-saving surgical procedures for various fractures now include pinning or screwing together the broken bones. Many horses have returned to active competition following surgery and rest.

Radiographs can confirm the diagnosis.

Fractures can occur in any bone in the horse's body, but in racehorses, hunters, jumpers, and eventers, most fractures occur in the front limbs because of the concussion and weight-bearing stress placed on them.

A veterinarian should be contacted immediately if such a serious leg problem is suspected. The vet can make a definitive diagnosis followed by surgical repair or another treatment program.

The good news is that equine bones often heal very rapidly and, once healed, are as strong as ever. The general time frame for a fracture to heal, if there are no other complications, is about four months. Removal of chip fractures does not require as much recuperative time, largely due to the development of arthroscopic techniques.

The following list describes some of the most common fractures:

Condylar fracture — Racehorses suffer this type of fracture, sometimes from the heavy stress placed on their left forelegs.

A condylar fracture occurs at the condyle, or lower knobby end of the cannon bone. Sometimes the bone fragment is broken away from the cannon bone. If it is broken away, it is called a complete fracture. If it isn't broken away, it is termed an incomplete fracture. Condylar fractures are treated surgically by using screws to compress the broken bone against the main bone.

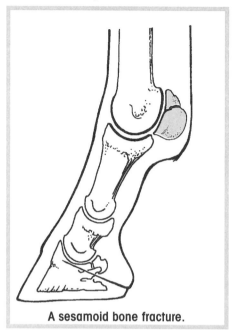

A sesamoid bone fracture.

Cortical Fracture — These are stress fractures of the front of the cannon bone. Screws generally are used in the repair process.

Cannon Bone Fracture — This is a catastrophic fracture that results in the bone literally breaking in two. Sometimes foals may be saved, but the prognosis is bleak for an adult horse.

Sagittal Fracture — Such a fracture occurs in the long pastern bone (first phalanx or P1). It is a fracture that runs down the pastern bone and can be either complete or incomplete. If there are bone fragments, they are removed surgically and a cast is placed on the injured pastern.

Coffin Bone Fracture — This type of fracture can take two forms: a sagittal fracture, which is right down the middle of the bone, or a "wing" fracture, when an inside or outside wing of the coffin bone breaks. Surgery is rarely an option in treating this type of fracture. Immobilizing the foot with a cast, then fitting it with special shoes and sole pads, is generally the best treatment approach.

Elbow Fracture — This type of fracture is more apt to occur in foals and weanlings than in adult horses. Such a fracture often results from a kick or a fall while at play. Technically, that portion of the elbow where the injury occurs is known as the olecranon. A plate attached by screws sometimes is used in treating this kind of fracture.

Knockdown Hip — This type of fracture can occur when a horse slams its hip against a door jamb or other immovable object. The pelvic structure, known as the ilium, is the part that fractures. Generally, such an injury heals on its own.

Splint Bone Fracture — This type of fracture is not uncommon and usually doesn't compromise the horse's athletic future. Often, such fractures are allowed to heal on their own, but this can result in an unsightly bump at the fracture site. The other option is to remove the fragmented end of bone surgically.

Sesamoid Bone Fracture — A fracture of the proximal sesamoids often can result from fatigue near the end of a race. Most fractured sesamoids occur in the forelegs of Thoroughbreds and in Quarter Horses when they race. In Standardbred racehorses, such fractures are found most often in the rear legs. If more than one-third of the bone has been fractured, the prognosis for recovery to form is poor. Treatment generally involves surgery to remove bone fragments and the use of surgical screws to piece the bone together.

Fetlock Joint Chip Fractures —These are fractures that often occur at the top or proximal end of the long pastern bone. The fractures generally occur as the result of concussion or over-extension of the fetlock joint. Arthroscopic surgery often is used to remove the fragments.

Carpal (knee) Fractures — The radial and third carpal bones are the ones most commonly fractured. However, chip fractures of the intermediate carpal bone and the radius might occur. In many cases, over-exertion of the limb is the cause of carpal fractures. Treatment involves removal of the bone chips or surgical fixation of the fragments with bone screws.

Microfractures — These tiny fissures in the bone result from wear and tear during strenuous exercise. Sometimes the wear and tear outstrip the body's ability to repair the damage. Then microfractures occur. If the bone is not given an opportunity to remodel or repair, the microfractures can lead to a much more serious fracture later on.

Joint injuries

This chapter and the previous one have touched on some joint injuries and afflictions that can result in lameness. Generally speaking, all joint injuries involve synovitis — injury to and inflammation of the synovial membrane — and capsulitis, the inflammation of the capsule itself. The two conditions go hand in hand. Both synovitis and capsulitis are common in horses which are involved in strenuous competition.

Symptoms include swelling and pain in the joints. If treated effectively when the conditions are first noticed, synovitis and capsulitis can be alleviated and the horse can return to competition. The danger is that the condition will persist and lead to a degenerative process in the joints — osteoarthritis.

Acute synovitis and capsulitis can be treated with cold packs or ice to reduce inflammation, the use of anti-inflammatory drugs, such as phenylbutazone, Banamine, and aspirin, and the administration of hyaluronic acid, either systemically or via injection directly into the joint.

Another weapon against joint disease is polysulfated glycosaminoglycans (Adequan). This therapy normally has been used where articular cartilage damage is suspected, rather than in the treatment of acute synovitis.

Corticosteroids also are used to combat joint injury as well as synovitis and capsulitis. However, their use is controversial. Some horse people maintain that corticosteroids contribute to degeneration of the joint because they inhibit pain, allowing the horse to continue to compete and, in the process, cause additional damage to the afflicted joint.

Recent research has indicated that, if administered properly, corticosteroids can be effective in combatting joint injuries, synovitis, and capsulitis without such deleterious side effects.

A variety of fractures can occur within the joints. In the past, they often meant an end to the horse's career or life, but the advent of arthroscopic surgery has changed that. It has become an effective tool in dealing with fractures within the joint.

This list of problems that can cause lameness is in no way a complete list, but the ones discussed are some of the most common problems.

Laminitis and navicular disease are two major causes of lameness that will be described separately because the two maladies affect so many horses and are quite different.

CHAPTER 6

Laminitis and Navicular Disease

Laminitis and navicular disease are two afflictions that can greatly undermine a horse's use. Both can cripple a horse. While laymen and professionals alike know how these two kinds of foot problems can affect horses, there remains a great deal of mystery about the causes, especially in the case of laminitis.

Laminitis also is referred to as founder. It can strike any breed and at any age. Its victims can range from the old backyard horse to the mighty Secretariat, who could conquer nearly all foes on the track, but could not defeat laminitis.

Millions of dollars have been spent on research, but there is still much that is unknown about the disease's cause, effect, and treatment; especially which treatment is most successful at various stages of the disease.

Many of the lameness problems described in this book have poor conformation at their root. The same is true for navicular disease, but it is not true with laminitis. There are many known causes of laminitis. There are also many laminitis cases where the cause is unknown.

A study done in the large animal clinic of Texas A&M University showed a total of 525 horses suffering from laminitis were admitted between 1978 to 1987. Data was collected to report the cause of each case of laminitis, but nearly half of the cases, 253 studies, listed "unknown" as the reported cause.

Grain overload was listed as the reported cause in 64 of the cases and gastrointestinal problems, such as colic and diarrhea, were close behind with 60 cases. Other laminitis cases included 34 caused by trauma and 30 cases attributed to road founder. Pasture founder accounted for 20 cases and pulmonary disease for 10 cases. Reported causes that were in the single digits included poor hoof trimming, drug-induced laminitis, hoof infection, systemic infection, moldy hay, metritis, deworming, water ingestion, edema, alfalfa hay, and myositis, an inflammation of a muscle.

> ## AT A GLANCE
>
> • Laminitis is an inflammation of the sensitive laminae in the horse's foot.
>
> • Laminitis can strike any horse at any age and can have crippling or fatal consequences.
>
> • Much remains unknown about the cause and effects of laminitis.

Another study from Texas A&M indicated that heredity might play a role in laminitis. The research involved a ranch-bred herd of Quarter Horses which were bred, broke, trained, and raced under the direct management of the owner.

Two genetic lines had been used heavily for five generations. Of 21 horses in one genetic line, a total of eight — one male and seven females — developed clinical signs consistent with chronic laminitis. Over the same period, only one horse in the other line displayed clinical signs consistent with laminitis.

In the group with the most afflicted horses, there was a similarity in their symptoms. In each case, the gradual onset of laminitis began after the horse was at least three years old. Several of the affected horses were racing when the first evidence of lameness developed; others had retired from racing and were being used as broodmares. The first physical evidence consisted of a gradual collapse of the dorsal walls of the front hooves, followed by the dropping of the soles and mild lameness. As their lameness increased in severity, the horses assumed the stance associated with laminitis — rocking back on their rear legs to alleviate the weight on their front feet.

The one horse from the other bloodline that had developed laminitis displayed different symptoms. In that case, the horse became instantly and severely lame when laminitis struck.

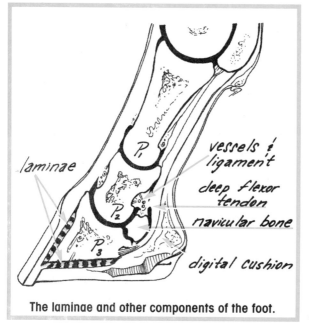

The laminae and other components of the foot.

Whatever the cause or its tendency to follow family lines, when acute laminitis strikes, changes take place in the sensitive area within the hard, horny hoof wall and the horse will display symptoms of severe pain. These problems can be so severe that they render the horse unable to perform again and can cause its death for humane reasons due to irreversable effects.

Laminitis has been compared to a human having a blood blister beneath a fingernail. Simply put, laminitis involves a disturbance in the circulation within the hoof and in the sensitive laminae which connect the horse's coffin bone (third phalanx) to the laminae of the inner hoof.

We might visualize the laminae, which hold the coffin bone

in place, as a web made of very strong Velcro that stabilizes the inner hoof structure as it connects the coffin bone to the interior of the hoof wall. When laminitis strikes, the sensitive laminae at the toe die shortly after the onset of the disease. The horny laminae of the hoof wall then separate from the sensitive laminae of the coffin bone.

Without the laminae holding it firmly in place, the coffin bone will rotate or sink, or do both. In severe cases, the point of the bone might even penetrate all the way through the sole. When that occurs, infection sets in and the horse's life is at risk.

There are two classifications of laminitis: acute, which is preceded by a developmental stage, and chronic.

Generally speaking, acute laminitis should be treated as a medical emergency. Chronic laminitis produces a lingering lameness that severely limits a horse's usefulness and follows in the wake of acute laminitis.

Signs of acute laminitis are well documented. There will be heat in the foot and a strong digital pulse. The horse will be in severe pain. Trying to alleviate that pain, the horse will stand with its front feet extended, rocking back on its rear feet and drawing them beneath its body for support.

The pain results from the inflammation within the sensitive structures in the horse's feet that are surrounded by the inflexible hoof wall.

Although laminitis normally strikes in the front feet, it also can affect the rear.

Acute laminitis is preceded by a developmental stage. Developmental laminitis occurs in that period between initiation of a systemic insult or insults that result in the disease and the appearance of acute lameness. Unfortunately, the horse normally shows few outward signs during the developmental phase of the disease.

Based on research done at Texas A&M, the developmental

phase usually lasts a maximum of 72 hours. It is followed by acute laminitis, with the onset of lameness and ends with the collapse of the structures within the hooves.

If the inner structures of the hooves do not collapse, the acute phase will end in about another 72 hours and the healing process will begin.

Unfortunately, the horse is often in the acute stage of laminitis before exhibiting any symptoms that would tip off an owner or handler. Once the disease moves from the developmental to the acute stage, damage within the hooves usually happens very rapidly.

As early as four hours after the first signs of lameness, cells within the feet swell. Red blood cell congestion and obstruction of the laminar capillaries begin within eight hours. Severe edema appears within 24 hours, and with it comes increased pain.

Damage to the laminae occurs as early as eight hours after lameness. It once was widely accepted that damage within the feet was linked to increased blood flow of such volume that the tiny capillaries and veins couldn't handle it. Now, many researchers believe that the opposite condition might occur. They call it ischemia, or reduced blood flow.

Researchers have put forward three theories to explain ischemia. One theory is that when laminitis is in the developmental stage, veins constrict within the feet. This causes swelling as the result of more fluid being moved through the capillaries. According to this theory, the resulting edema is trapped behind the hoof wall, which increases tissue pressure and further decreases blood flow.

A second theory contends that ischemic necrosis (the death of cells) and associated pain occurs because the blood is being shunted away from the laminae.

The third theory is the one held by the Texas A&M researchers. They contend that laminitis results from peripheral vasospasm (a spasm of the blood vessels, resulting in a decrease of their blood-carrying capability) which results in a curtailment of blood flow within the foot.

When the vasospasm is over, there is an increased blood flow beyond what would be normal. This problem, by itself, can be harmful and painful.

According to the researchers, the duration and intensity of the vasospasm determines the intensity of clinical signs. If the episode is mild, the horse will have a stronger digital pulse, an increase in temperature in the hooves, and some pain when blood flow returns.

The researchers theorized that the collapse of the structures within the feet occurs when the vasospasms are severe. The stoppage of blood flow, followed by its return in greater than normal quantities, causes severe tissue injury.

Their theory appears plausible. There is no pain during the absence of blood flow. By comparison, the effect on the horse of the reduced blood flow is similar to what happens when a person's foot "goes to sleep." There is no feeling during the stoppage of blood flow that results in numbness, but there is a tingling sensation when blood flow returns.

Whatever the cause, laminitis cases need immediate veterinary attention. To date, there has been no single treatment that is 100% successful in combating acute laminitis. The goal is to reduce pain and to prevent laminitis from reaching the chronic stage. When drugs have been given to horses in the early stages of the disease, there has been some success reported.

The acute stage is brief, generally ranging from four to 60 hours. However, because of the short time horses spend in the acute stage of laminitis, most are already in the chronic phase when they are treated by a veterinarian.

The treatment of choice advocated by the Texas A&M researchers involves the use of pain medications such as phenylbutazone and Banamine, along with drugs that will tend to dilate veins and capillaries, such as phenoxybenzamine and acepromazine. The use of drugs should be accompanied by advice to give the horse complete stall rest.

This treatment protocol must include treating the cause of the laminitis attack if it is known, for example, treatment of colic or metritis.

Rehabilitating a horse with chronic laminitis can be difficult. Again, there is no single method that is best. Each patient with chronic laminitis must be treated as an individual. For example, the treatment protocol should include asking the farrier to take extra care with the horse's trimming and shoeing program.

Much more is known about laminitis today than a decade ago, but a great many mysteries remain to be solved. How to prevent laminitis is the most mysterious problem. If over-eating were its only cause, for example, limiting the horse's food intake would eliminate the problem.

Unfortunately, there are myriad known and unknown causes of laminitis.

Hopefully, continued research will solve the mysteries of laminitis soon. Until then, an owner's best course is to get their horses prompt treatment when laminitis occurs.

NAVICULAR DISEASE

As is the case with laminitis, a fair amount of mystery surrounds navicular disease. One thing is sure: any horse with navicular disease, or navicular syndrome, is a lame horse.

The navicular bone is located in the middle of the hoof on the bottom side of the coffin joint, at the point where the coffin bone (P3) joins with the short pastern bone (second phalanx, P2). It acts something like a pulley. Its prime function is to allow the force distributed through the deep digital flexor tendon to change directions as it passes over the navicular bone and attaches to the coffin bone. The navicular bone is supported in its position by three ligaments. The articular surface of the navicular bone is covered with a hyaline cartilage. The navicular bursa lies between the deep digital flexor tendon and the navicular bone and provides a synovial-filled gliding surface between bone and tendon.

The navicular bone is not rounded like a true pulley where the greatest pressure would be applied to the middle. Instead, the navicular bone is somewhat triangular, with the deep digital flexor tendon crossing it at the bottom (distal) surface. Because it is square, the tendon crossing it is going to

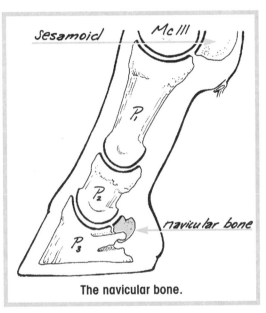

The navicular bone.

apply more pressure to the distal border of the flexor surface. Most navicular problems arise at this location. (The flexor surface is that area of the navicular bone in contact with the deep digital flexor tendon and the distal border is the lower third of the flexor surface.)

Horses with navicular disease often have a short, shuffling gait and a history of intermittent lameness. In many cases, the shuffling gait is misdiagnosed as a shoulder problem.

Navicular disease normally affects both front feet. However, it is not unusual for one of the feet to be more severely impacted than the other.

A horse with navicular problems often will stand with one front toe pointed down, resting almost no weight on its most painful foot. If both front feet are equally involved, the horse will point one foot first, then the other; or it will stand with both front feet camped out in front.

When it moves, the navicular horse often will alter its gait by trying to land on its toe or flatly on each foot in an effort to lessen the concussion in the heel area. The nerves in the bulb of the heel carry the message: PAIN! The pain also might cause the horse to stumble at the walk or trot. The symptoms are more noticeable when the horse is turning in a circle.

In many instances, the cause of navicular disease is poor conformation. For example, horses with upright pasterns and horses with tiny hooves supporting their large, bulky bodies are prone to navicular disease.

Improper trimming, shoeing, or absence of foot mass also cause navicular disease. Horses which are trimmed or shod with long toes and low heels are predisposed to navicular disease.

Pathological findings from autopsies of horses with navicular disease have been inconsistent.

As is the case with laminitis, there are a number of theories about what happens within the foot when navicular disease strikes. There is, for example, the bursitis theory. Proponents of this theory believe that inflammation of the navicular bursa, as the result of concussion, can lead to alteration of the flexor surface of the bone.

Then, there is the thrombosis-and-ischemia theory. Some researchers claim that navicular problems arise when a thrombosis, or obstruction, occurs in the arteries of the foot. When this results in ischemia (lack of blood flow), necrosis of the bone follows.

A somewhat similar theory is the arthrosis theory. Proponents say increased pressures within the navicular bone follow in the wake of a curtailment of blood flow through the veins.

The most widely held theory is the bone-remodeling theory. Proponents believe that the navicular bone goes through an abnormal bone-remodeling process when concussion and other forces are brought to bear. It works something like this: Compression of cartilage as a result of these forces leads to cartilage necrosis, or death of cartilage cells. When that happens, the bone just beneath the cartilage, the subchondral bone, becomes very dense. Such pressures cause the navicular bone to remodel.

> ## AT A GLANCE
>
> • Navicular disease involves the navicular bone in the foot.
>
> • Navicular disease can produce varying degrees of lameness. It often manifests itself in a short, shuffling gait.
>
> • Poor conformation, shoeing, or both can contribute to navicular disease.

Remodeling involves two types of cells: osteoclast and osteoblast. Though the names are similar, their actions are not. Osteoclasts tear down bone and osteoblasts rebuild bone, or remodel it.

This is a normal procedure in bones. For example, broken bones begin to mend when the body signals that present bone cells are to be discarded and new bone that is thicker and stronger is to be constructed.

This process might have a negative effect on the navicular bone. When the deep digital flexor tendon exerts undue pressure on the cartilage, it dies. As pressure continues, the bone gets the signal that it needs to be stronger. The osteoclasts are set in motion and they begin tearing down the weakened structure and the osteoblasts begin building a stronger one. In response to the unremitting pressure, sometimes the osteoclasts tear down more than the osteoblasts can rebuild and a hole soon appears in the bone. Then, granulation tissue begins to cover the surface of the navicular bone. It eventually adheres to the deep digital flexor tendon. When that happens, the horse becomes very lame.

Such abnormal pressure on the navicular bone is often the result of poor conformation. Upright pasterns increase the amount of concussion absorbed within the foot. The concussion harms the navicular bone.

Whenever a horse's foot is trimmed or shod in order to have a long toe and low heel, the amount of pressure exerted against the navicular bone by the deep digital flexor tendon is increased dramatically. If the horse also has upright pasterns, the problem has been exaggerated.

Still another cause of navicular disease is a condition known as sheared heels. Poor trimming or shoeing can leave the horse with heels of uneven length, resulting in an imbalance. To check a horse in order to identify sheared heels, place it with both front feet on a hard, level surface, and then examine them from the rear by comparing the distance from the hairline to the ground on each heel bulb. If one is longer than the other, there will be a definite shearing action in the frog and navicular areas of the foot. The problem will be compounded if the horse is heavy, or if it frequently is asked to travel at speed, especially over a hard surface.

Sheared heels should be addressed through a corrective trimming and shoeing program.

Diagnosing navicular disease is not always easy, even with the use of radiographs. X-rays of older horses show a certain amount of normal wear and tear in the navicular region that resembles, and sometimes masks, the problems resulting from navicular disease. In addition to taking X-rays, a veterinarian will use a hoof tester and perhaps nerve blocks in an effort to determine a definitive diagnosis.

The prognosis for a horse with navicular disease is always guarded. Much depends on how much bone damage has occurred and whether corrective shoeing and medication have been attempted.

PROPER TRIMMING AND SHOEING ESSENTIAL

The first order of treatment is to restore correct balance to the foot through proper trimming and shoeing. The fact that proper trimming and shoeing can help was proven in a University of Florida study of 48 horses with navicular disease. Some of the horses had just gone lame and others had been lame for as many as five years. In each case, the existing hoof problems were corrected with proper trimming and shoeing. Then, the horses in the study were placed into three groups. The 29 horses in the largest group were used in riding classes involving Western and English riding and dressage. The second group consisted of eight horses used in stressful events such as barrel racing, cutting, gymkhana, and roping. The 11 horses in the third group were used over fences as hunters or jumpers.

All three groups were kept on a routine exercise program that included at least 30 minutes of regular work under saddle six days a week. In all three groups, the shoeing program had improved the way of going when the horses were checked 90 days into the study. The total testing period for each horse ranged from six to 54 months, depending on the individuals. Overall, proper shoeing successfully managed the lameness in 36 of the 48 horses with navicular disease. Two of the horses were sound for one year. In five cases, the shoeing technique was not successful.

The study also described another finding that horse owners should keep in mind. Thirty of the horses involved had been treated within 10 months of the first sign of lameness; 29 of them remained sound. Of the 13 horses that had been lame for a year or longer, only seven remained sound. Therefore, if a navicular problem is suspected, it should be given immediate attention.

Palmar digital neurectomy, better known among laymen as "nerving," is something of a court of last resort when dealing with navicular disease. It is a surgical procedure in which a section of the nerve is removed, thus alleviating pain. This procedure does not produce a lasting cure, but in some cases, it might yield a few more years of use. However, it does nothing to solve the problem, or cure the disease. In fact, it could worsen the problem because after nerving, a horse can no longer feel the pain that caused it to alleviate pressure and concussion on the affected foot.

In most cases, this procedure is recommended only after all other attempted remedies have failed.

It usually is easier to prevent navicular disease than to cure it. First and foremost, proper trimming and shoeing helps. Second, and this is perhaps a more subtle point, horses with upright pasterns should not be used in disciplines that create a great deal of concussion. Third, when a horse shows signs of diminished performance and its stride appears different, it should be examined immediately by a veterinarian. The Florida study proved that early detection, immediate treatment, and an appropriate trimming and shoeing program are critically important when navicular disease strikes.

Horses should be trimmed every six to eight weeks as a navicular preventive measure. The hoof wall at the toe and heel don't always grow at the same rate. In addition, the horse's foot grows forward. Therefore, if there is more rapid growth at the toe than the heel, the horse very soon will have a foot that predisposes it to navicular disease.

Poorly shod horses often are fitted with shoes that are too

small and do not provide adequate support. This practice also might predispose the horses to navicular disease. To provide the needed support, which will help the foot to break forward instead of dropping backward, the shoe should extend beyond the heel. The nails also should be placed so that the horse's foot can expand when it is in motion. This means that nails should not be placed past the bend in the quarters.

CHAPTER 7

Diagnosing Lameness

Diagnosing the causes of lameness problems can range from easy to impossible. When a horse hobbles across the pasture with blood dripping from a wire cut, we know instantly why it is lame. If a horse shows signs of a subtle, intermittent lameness and its slightly diminished performance is the only clue, finding the cause might be difficult.

Fortunately for the 20th Century horse owner, a number of tools, some of them very sophisticated, are available to assist in determining the cause in most cases. Veterinarians can use anesthesia (nerve blocks), radiographs, ultrasound, scintigraphy, thermography, arthroscopy, muscle biopsy, and high-speed photography to help them determine the cause of lameness.

Horse owners or trainers can provide basic information to the veterinarian, who in turn can do a more sophisticated analysis.

There are three basic questions to ask in order to diagnose lameness: 1) Which limb is involved or are there more than one contributing to the lameness? 2) Where exactly in that foot or leg is the seat of lameness? 3) What is the cause?

Unfortunately, there are no simple answers for the three questions. Take the first, for example. We might look at the horse and determine that the lameness is in the left foreleg. But, is it really? The problem might have originated in a rear leg or in another part of the skeletal structure that caused the horse to carry more weight in front, producing soreness. Yes, the left front might show signs of lameness, but after it is treated, the horse will soon be lame on the left foreleg once again if the cause goes undiscovered. In this case, lameness is the symptom, the soreness in the rear or skeletal problems are the causes.

All three questions are interconnected. It often takes a veterinarian to unravel the mystery and arrive at a definitive diagnosis.

The American Association of Equine Practitioners (AAEP) has established a "Definition and Classification of Lameness," which many veterinarians use in describing various conditions.

The AAEP guideline uses the following classifications:

• Grade 1 - Difficult to observe; not consistently apparent regardless of circumstances (i.e., weight carrying, circling, inclines, hard surfaces, etc.).

• Grade 2 - Difficult to observe at a walk or trotting a straight line; consistently apparent under certain circumstances (i.e., weight carrying, circling, inclines, hard surfaces, etc.).

• Grade 3 - Consistently observable at a trot under all circumstances.

• Grade 4 - Obvious lameness; marked nodding, hitching or

AT A GLANCE

• Diagnosing lameness might require only observation; other times, it might require the use of sophisticated equipment.

• Lameness is graded on a scale of one to five, with five being the most severe.

• Lameness can involve more than one leg.

• An owner or handler can assist the veterinarian in determining the cause of the lameness by knowing what is normal or abnormal in the particular horse.

• Alternative approaches such as acupuncture and physical therapy can be useful in determining lameness.

a shortened stride.

• Grade 5 - Minimal weight bearing in motion and/or at rest; inability to move.

There are more lamenesses in the forelegs than in the hindquarters because horses bear more weight on their front legs. Therefore, their forelegs are subjected to greater concussion than their hindquarters, which are used more for propulsion.

In an estimated 95% of front leg lamenesses, the source is in the area from the knee down through the foot. There are lamenesses involving the forearm, elbow, and shoulder, but they are far fewer in number.

If the lameness is in a rear leg, the cause is most apt to be located in the hock.

DETERMINING THE LAMENESS

When attempting to diagnose lameness, one should start at the ground level and work up the horse's legs, examining and eliminating potential sites until the cause is identified.

Watching the horse at rest in its stall is a good way to begin the examination. How does it stand? Is it holding one foreleg forward in a pointing fashion? If so, the pointed foot might be an early warning sign of navicular disease. Does the horse stand with one back foot cocked, resting that foot on the toe? It is common for horses to cock one rear foot or the other, but if it always cocks the same one and is reluctant to put weight on that limb, it could be a clue to a lameness problem in that particular foot or leg. Does the horse stand with both front feet angled forward from its body? That's another sign that the horse might have navicular problems in both front feet. Is it rocking back on the rear legs in an effort to take its weight off its front feet? That is the classic stance of a horse suffering from laminitis.

Experts describe and classify lameness in the following four basic ways:

Supporting Leg Lameness — This is a lameness that occurs whenever the horse is supporting weight on the foot or when it lands on the foot.

Swinging Leg Lameness — This kind of lameness is evident when the leg is in motion and often involves joint capsules, tendons, and muscles.

Mixed Leg Lameness — Now things become more complicated. In this category, lameness is evident both in the supporting and swinging phases.

Complementary Lameness — This occurs whenever the lameness in one limb causes another limb to become sore and compromised until it, too, shows signs of lameness.

Observing the horse in motion carries the diagnosis beyond a look for the signature head nodding that indicates foreleg lamenesses or the raising of one side of the croup that might indicate rear limb lameness. Studying the horse's stride is imperative. There are two phases to each stride: the front, or anterior, phase and the rear, or posterior, phase.

When the horse travels, if either phase is shortened it indicates problems in that limb. For example, a horse with a shortened anterior phase and a lengthened posterior phase in a rear limb might be trying to show it has a hock problem, perhaps a spavin, or that its problem might involve the stifle.

The path of the foot in flight also can indicate the location of a specific problem. If a horse wings in, for example, interference is likely to be the cause of its lameness.

How the foot lands also is significant. For example, if a horse is suffering from navicular disease, it will attempt to land on its toe rather than its heel in order to lessen painful concussion. Conversely, a horse with a problem in the toe area will attempt to land on the heel area of the foot.

Flexion tests (by flexing and bending the limbs) also can help to diagnose a specific problem. A horse which shows definite lameness after its hock is held in a flexed position for a minute or more might indicate that it is suffering from a bone spavin.

Knowing the history of each horse, particularly the ways it has been used, is invaluable in diagnosing lameness because different disciplines bring different stresses and pressures to bear on the horse. A Thoroughbred is most apt to be afflicted with joint, tendon, and ligament problems while a stock horse which is competing in barrel racing, roping, reining, and cutting is more apt to suffer from bone spavin, ringbone, sidebone, and fractures involving the pastern bones.

Veterinarians often use hoof testers to determine the site of lameness in the foot. (Hoof testers resemble the old-fashioned clamps icemen used to carry blocks of ice.) When pressure is applied to a sore area of a horse's sole, it will cause more pain and the horse will flinch.

Local injections to anesthetize portions of the foot or segments of the leg are called nerve blocks. A series of such injections can help pinpoint the site of a lameness problem. In this procedure, the veterinarian normally starts at the bottom and works up. When a specific area of the foot or leg has been deadened with the anesthetic, if the horse remains lame, then at least one potential site has been eliminated. When a nerve block in a specific area renders the horse temporarily sound, it is a strong indication that the problem site has been identified.

Palpation is an option that a horse owner can try. Just as the term implies, palpation involves examining the animal by touch, running one's hands up and down the limbs, feeling for any abnormality. If a front leg is involved, one would examine that leg and also the one that is sound in order to determine what, if any, deviation can be felt in the lame leg.

Palpation is an excellent initial step to determine if there is inflammation. Inflammation is synonymous with heat. It can be felt with the fingers or back of the hand by comparing the heat in the affected limb with that of the opposite, unaffected limb.

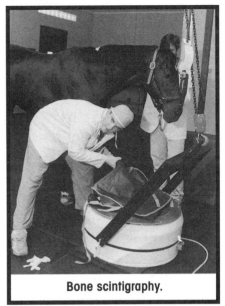

Bone scintigraphy.

Once the problem area is known, radiographs might be employed if a bony lesion is suspected.

OTHER DIAGNOSTIC TOOLS

There are also a number of other diagnostic options available to the equine community:

Ultrasound — If the lameness problem involves a tendon, ultrasound can be an invaluable tool. It is a technique using sound waves to provide information about the structure of the tendon or other soft tissues. It can be particularly useful, for example, in monitoring the recovery process of a horse with a bowed tendon.

Scintigraphy — If the problem appears to be in a bone and radiographs do not produce a definitive diagnosis, the veterinarian might turn to bone scintigraphy for the answer. It involves an intravenous administration of radioactive material followed by an examination of the affected area with a scintillation counter, which records radiation in picture form. Areas where there is increased radioactivity indicate bone growth, active bone damage, or fracture healing.

Thermography — This technique involves graphic imaging of the temperature differences in the skin. Thermography can be particularly useful when a problem is suspected, but no clinical signs have appeared. For example, if the temperature in the forearm of the horse's left front leg is higher than that of the opposite leg, it could be a tipoff that a lameness problem is looming.

High-speed photography — This diagnostic tool involves using extremely high-speed film to shoot pictures of a horse's legs while it is traveling on a treadmill. Because of the many frames shot at high speed, the horse's gait can be analyzed in minute fashion in every phase of each stride.

Muscle biopsy — When a muscle problem is suspected, a sample is removed surgically, then analyzed to determine if problems exist within that particular muscle.

Exploratory arthroscopy — Arthroscopic surgery is employed to remove bone chips from joints. Endoscopy of joints also enables the practitioner to evaluate accurately the synovial membrane, articular cartilage, and intra-articular ligaments.

Synovial fluid analysis — Collection and analysis of fluid from a joint can provide useful information about various problems within the joint. A synovial fluid analysis can guide the practitioner in determining whether the problem involves an infection or is the result of trauma.

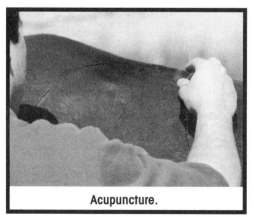
Acupuncture.

Alternative approaches — A number of veterinarians today are making use of both acupuncture and chiropractic in the diagnosis and treatment of lameness. Acupuncture has been a treatment of choice for many years in some cultures and today is being used increasingly in the equine veterinary world. It involves key sensitive points on a horse's body that often can lead the practitioner to the cause of lameness and also provide an avenue for treatment.

Equine chiropractic is also on the increase. Some lamenesses stem from causes that can be treated by an adjustment from an equine chiropractor. It is important when using alternative approaches that the horse owner seek out a practitioner who has been properly trained in employing the modality on equines.

Therapy with ultrasound.

This normally means a veterinarian who has added the approaches to his or her repertoire.

Not every practitioner will have immediate access to all of the diagnostic techniques and tools listed above. Some of the equipment is extremely expensive and can only be found at major equine hospitals or research facilities. Such institutions make their tools and techniques available to solve difficult lameness problems. Remember that new technological advances and lameness research will continue to provide answers to the most troubling lameness questions.

CHAPTER 8
Preventing Lameness

Some lamenesses are preventable. The opportunity to avoid lameness problems often starts when a prospective owner asks a veterinarian to do a pre-purchase examination on a horse. Such an examination is especially important when you are considering the purchase of a performance or breeding animal.

The American Association of Equine Practitioners suggests the following guidelines:

(1) Choose a veterinarian who is familiar with the breed, sport, or use for which the horse is being purchased.

(2) Before the exam, explain to the veterinarian how you plan to use the horse. Explain your expectations, including short- and long-term goals. For example, the goals might be showing the horse for a few years, then breeding it.

(3) Ask your veterinarian to outline the procedures that will be included in the examination — and why they are important.

(4) Get a cost estimate for such procedures. The expense of the exam and related lab work is sure to be small in comparison with the long-term costs of caring for a horse, especially one with health problems.

(5) Be present for the exam. Because the seller, or agent also should be present, ask the veterinarian to give you his or her findings in private.

(6) Do not be afraid to ask questions or request further information about the veterinarian's findings.

The veterinarian's job is not either to pass or fail the animal. The vet acts as your adviser, but you are the only one who can make the decision to purchase the horse, or pass it up.

If you doubt the veterinarian's finding during the pre-purchase

AT A GLANCE

- Before buying a horse, have it examined by a veterinarian.

- Choose the right horse for the particular discipline.

- Provide the horse with a safe environment to reduce the risk of injury.

- Provide the horse with professional foot care on a routine basis.

exam, get a second opinion. Be sure to select a veterinarian who has experience doing pre-purchase equine examinations and who does not do business with the seller.

Remember that no horse is perfect in every respect. Some medical conditions and some conformation faults are manageable. Depending on the level of performance you expect, some conformation faults might not seriously affect the horse.

While there is no standard protocol of procedures for a pre-purchase examination, the veterinarian often starts by evaluating the horse's conformation and observing the horse' behavior; then watching the horse travel in a straight line, in small circles, and under saddle, preferably at the walk, trot, and canter, and preferably before the horse has been warmed up.

Following that portion of the examination, the veterinarian is likely to do the following:

- Monitor pulse, respiration, and temperature.
- Listen to the heart and lungs.
- Check nostrils, ears, and eyes.

• Palpate body and limbs.
• Examine teeth and mouth.
• Evaluate feet visually and with hoof testers.
• Perform flexion tests on joints.
• Draw blood samples for Coggins and other tests.

If any of the items described above alerts the practitioner to existing or potential problems, he or she might recommend further tests before the purchase is made. Tests such as radiographs, nerve blocks, urine and blood analysis, and endoscopic and ultrasonic examinations might be recommended by the veterinarian.

A SAFE ENVIRONMENT

Once the purchase decision has been made and the horse arrives at its new home, there are several ways the horse owner can avoid lameness problems. Keeping horse pastures and paddocks free of potential hazards is a must.

Good fencing is important.

Injuries to feet and legs — problems such as puncture wounds and wire cuts — should go at the top of the list of preventable lameness problems.

Horses are naturally curious and have a tendency to check out everything in their environment. When a horse paws at a broken-down fence or at a roll of rusty barbed wire in an effort to satisfy its curiosity, the result might be a severely lacerated leg. Remember that a horse's first line of defense in most frightening situations is flight. If it gets a leg caught in wire and feels trapped, it will attempt to flee. If its leg is caught in the wire, the damage might be extensive.

Other avoidable hazards include sharp objects that are imbedded in the ground. If they are allowed to remain, it usually is just a matter of time until the horse ends up with a puncture wound.

Veterinarians say they are frequently called in to treat lameness problems that result from injuries that could have been prevented simply by keeping the horse's environment free of harmful objects and debris.

Avoiding the use of barbed wire to enclose horse pastures is a good preventive measure. Avoiding woven wire that has openings or squares large enough to trap a horse's foot is also a good preventive measure. In any herd, there is always one curious horse who paws at such fencing and winds up with a shoe caught on the wire and its foot held firmly in place. If the trapped horse panics, serious damage will result.

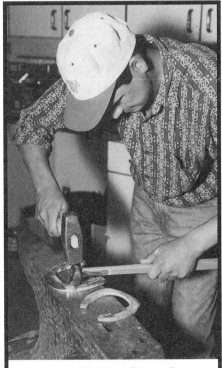

Horses' feet require regular maintenance.

TAKE CARE OF FEET AND LEGS

Appropriate fencing and a clean environment are two obvious approaches in the prevention of lameness. Perhaps not quite as obvious, but just as important, is continual attention to the feet and legs. Doing something as simple as cleaning the feet with a hoof pick before riding might prevent a bruise if a stone has become lodged in the dirt and debris that sometimes forms a solid pack on the bottom of the foot. Regular cleaning is also the best way to prevent thrush.

Then, there is the matter of timely trimming and shoeing. All too often the casual horse owner is diligent about trimming and shoeing during the active riding months, but forgets about it during the winter. It is true that hooves grow more slowly during cold weather, but they still grow and should be maintained.

As a general rule, a horse's hooves should be trimmed or shod every four to six weeks. There will be variations in this rule of thumb because all hooves do not grow at the same rate. But if one goes beyond six to eight weeks, generally speaking, the horse will be wearing a hoof that is too long for its comfort and good health.

Another part of the lameness prevention picture involves the ground on which a horse is pastured. If it spends most of its time on soft, spongy ground, or if it's stuck in a box stall for many hours per day, there will be little wear on the hooves. When a horse is pastured on hard rocky ground, where grass is sparse and there are long treks to water, it will pretty much serve as its own farrier. The travel, combined with the unyielding ground, will wear away excess growth from its hooves. That is the case with range-bred horses and wild bands.

A great many domesticated horses spend most of their lives in paddocks, small pastures, or stalls where the ground is forgiving and travel is all but unnecessary. Such conditions lead to steady hoof growth with no natural wear.

We have taken the horse out of its natural environment and ensconced it in ours. While moving it into an artificial environment helps us live close enough to the horse to enjoy and use it, horse ownership also brings with it a serious responsibility: to take proper care of the animal's feet and legs.

Just trimming or shoeing is not enough. It must be done properly. A horse owner either must become a capable farrier, or the owner must find a competent person to do the work. There are many good farriers in the horse world. Unfortunately, there are also some who are incompetent and do not understand the foot and leg anatomy of the horse.

Once a horse reaches a year or so of age, the window of opportunity for some types of corrective shoeing is over. To attempt corrective trimming on an adult horse that toes out, for example, will result in nothing more than putting undue stress on its entire support apparatus. Having the problem in the first place induces stress, but to seek correction of such a conformation defect adds to the stress factor and might induce lameness.

Trimming and shoeing techniques that break the pastern-foot axis of an adult horse are also a case of corrective shoeing (or trimming) applied too late. The hoof angle and the pastern angle must be the same if bones, tendons, and ligaments in that area of the leg and foot are to be aligned properly. If they are not — particularly if there is a long toe and low heel — too much stress can be placed on the navicular bone where the deep flexor tendon crosses it. Shaping a horse's feet in such a manner predisposes it to navicular disease, especially if the horse has upright pasterns.

All horse owners should make it a point to learn about the basic foot and leg anatomy of the horse. While the owners might not be capable of doing the shoeing and trimming, they should be educated to the point where they can recognize the kind of poor farrier work that can have a negative effect on the health and welfare of their horses.

APPROPRIATE USE

There is also the matter of putting a square peg in a square hole and a round peg in a round hole, instead of vice versa. Someone might own a horse which is a fine jumper. However, if that horse has extremely offset knees, its career as a jumper might be very short because its front legs will not stand up to the stress of landing jump after jump.

Another person might own the best-bred cutting horse or reining horse in the world, but if it has weak hocks, it is not going to last long in competitions where sliding stops and quick turns are required.

The key is first to decide what our goals are for the horse we are about to purchase or use, then find one with the conformation that fits that task. Finding the appropriate horse for a particular discipline is a must if the horse is to remain sound and serviceable.

Finally, there is the matter of observation and consciousness. Responsible horse owners quickly learn to pick up on the most minor, subtle changes they see or sense in their horses.

Is the horse just a tad off on that left rear today? Is there a bit of heat in the tendon as we run our fingers over it? Is the horse cocking its left rear more often today than it ever has before? Is it just a bit listless, when normally its ears are up and its eyes bright?

The horse will tell you when something is wrong. You simply have to be observant enough to pick up on it. There is no way you can become observant without concentration. Every time you bring your horse out of its stall, paddock, or pasture, you should be concentrating on whether everything is normal. You should take note of even a slight abnormality in the way it travels.

Before and after each competition or outing on the horse, its rider should check its ligaments and tendons for signs of heat and swelling. Being alert to a minor problem today can prevent a disaster tomorrow.

The horse's owner or trainer always must put its welfare first. Someone might want to enter a race, a jumping competition, or perhaps a reining class, only to discover just before the event that the horse is slightly lame.

There are several drugs and treatments that can eliminate the pain, so the horse appears to travel correctly without signs of lameness. However, such treatments effectively can mask what is truly wrong. For example, an injection might eliminate the sensation of pain temporarily from a minor tendon injury so the horse can compete and appear to be sound, but the horse might end up with a severe bow. Such an injury can compromise the horse's future ability to perform and endanger its survival.

Many horses are very competitive by nature. A racehorse which breaks its leg during a race might gallop on, desperately trying to reach the finish line. A cutting horse will attempt to stop a cow, even though its hocks are inflamed. A gaited horse will fire up and charge into the ring and attempt to perform even though its feet and legs are sore.

A good horse will give, and give some more, whenever and whatever we ask of it. It is our responsibility as owners to know when not to ask.

GLOSSARY

Amble — Gait that is similar to a pace at walking speed.

Arthroscopy — Using a surgical device to examine interior of joints.

Bench knee — Forearm and cannon bone are not properly aligned at knee.

Bog spavin — Inflammation of synovial lining of hock joint.

Bone spavin — Bony growth in hock joint.

Bowed tendon — Tendinitis of superficial and/or deep digital flexor tendons.

Brushing — General term for light striking, as in forging and interfering.

Buck knee — Front knee bends forward.

Bucked shins — Inflammation of tissue covering cannon bones.

Bursitis — Inflammation of the bursa.

Calf knee — A conformational fault in which the front knee bends backward.

Camped out — Rear legs located too far to the rear.

Cannon bone — Also known as metacarpus. Extends from knee to pastern.

Cannon fracture — Catastrophic breaking of cannon bone.

Canter or lope — A three-beat gait.

Capsulitis — Inflammation of the fibrous joint capsule.

Carpus — The knee.

Coffin bone — Also known as third phalanx. Located within hoof, connecting to bottom of short pastern bone or second phalanx.

Condylar fracture — One that travels up the cannon bone.

Conformation — The way in which a horse is constructed.

Corn — A form of bruise to sole of foot.

Cortical fracture — Stress fracture to front of cannon bone.

Cow-hocked: A horse with hocks closer together than are the feet.

Cross firing — Inside of hind foot hitting inside quarter of diagonal forefoot.

Croup — The pelvic area, beginning at end of spinal column and ending at tailhead.

Curb — Bowing or thickening of long plantar ligament in rear leg.

Deep digital flexor tendon — Passes over elbow and down leg to ultimately attach to coffin bone. Involved in flexing of joints.

Desmitis — Inflammation of a ligament.

Femur — The thigh bone which is connected to the pelvis.

First phalanx — Long pastern bone which connects to bottom of cannon bone.

Forging — Toe of hind foot hits sole area of forefoot on same side.

Fox trot — Horse appears to be walking in front and trotting in rear. Signature gait of the Missouri Fox Trotter.

Gallop — A four-beat gait with the horse traveling at speed.

Gravel — Infectious condition of white line of hoof.

High speed cinematography — Use of high speed cameras to photograph strides of a horse, usually on a treadmill.

Hock — Rear leg joint where tibia meets rear cannon bone.

Humerus — Bone that angles down from scapula and connects to radius.

Hyaluronic acid — An integral component of both synovial fluid and articular cartilage in normal joints.

Ilium — A horse's pelvis. Connects to spinal column.

Interfering — Striking of lower leg by opposite foot.

Joints — Area where bones join together.

Laminae — Tissue that connects the coffin bone to the inner hoof wall.

Laminitis — A serious affliction of the foot that can leave permanent damage.

Ligament — Band of tissue that connects the articular extremities. Ligaments also hold body organs in place.

Metacarpus — Also known as cannon bone. Extends from knee to pastern.

Metatarsus — Rear cannon bone running from hock to pastern.

Navicular bone — Also known as distal sesamoid. Located at juncture of short pastern bone and coffin bone.

Osselet — Traumatic arthritis of fetlock joint.

Osteitis — Inflammation of a bone.

Osteoarthritis — Progressive loss of articular cartilage on the surface of the bone.

Osteophytosis — Formation of a bony growth.

Overreaching — Toe of hind foot caches the forefoot on same side, usually striking the heel.

Pace — A two-beat gait with left front and left rear and right front and right rear moving in unison.

Periostitis — Inflammation of tissue that covers bone.

Pigeon toed — Conformational fault that has toes turned inward.

Plaiting — A horse which travels with one front foot placed directly in front of the other.

Proximal sesamoid bones — Located just behind cannon bone at juncture with long pastern bone. Serve as pulleys for deep flexor tendon.

Quittor — Inflammation of a collateral cartilage of coffin bone.

Rack — Similar to running walk, except there is no overreach.

Radius — Also known as the forearm. Extends downward to the knee.

Ringbone — Bony growth that can occur on long and short pastern bones and coffin bone.

Running walk — A four-cornered gait with each foot hitting the ground separately at regular intervals, with overreach from rear legs. Signature gait of Tennessee Walking Horse.

Sagittal fracture — Fracture to long pastern bone.

Scapula — Shoulder bone.

Scintigraphy — Intravenous injection of radioactive material to help locate bone problems.

Second phalanx — Short pastern bone that connects to bottom of long pastern bone.

Sesamoiditis — Inflammation of the proximal sesamoid bones.

Sickle-hocked — Rear legs angled too far forward from hocks down.

Sidebone — Ossification of cartilages of the coffin bone.

Speedy cutting — Any type of limb interference at fast gait.

Splint bones — Travel downward from knee on either side of cannon bone.

Splints — Bony growth between ligament and cannon bone along splint bones.

Standing under — Rear legs located too far forward.

Stifle — Similar to human knee. The point where femur and tibia meet.

Stringhalt — Involuntary flexion of rear hock.

Superficial flexor tendon — Extends from radius to attachment on long pastern bone or first phalanx. Involved in flexing of joints.

Synovial fluid — Lubrication within the joint.

Synovial membrane — Inner line of joint capsule that secretes synovial fluid.

Synovitis — Inflammation of the synovial membrane.

Tendinitis — Inflammation of a tendon.

Tendon — A tough cord or band of dense connective tissue that unites a muscle with some other part.

Thermography — Use of a heat device to diagnose lameness.

Third phalanx — Coffin bone. Connects to bottom of short pastern bone.

Thoroughpin — Inflammation of tarsal sheath just above the hock.

Thrush — Degenerative condition of frog.

Tibia — Bone running from femur to hock.

Toeing out — A conformational fault that has front feet turned outward.

Trot — A two-beat gait with front and rear limbs traveling as diagonal pairs.

Ultrasound — The use of sound waves to help diagnose lameness.

Walk — A four-beat gait with each foot hitting ground at a separate interval.

Windpuffs — Fluid-filled swellings around fetlock joint.

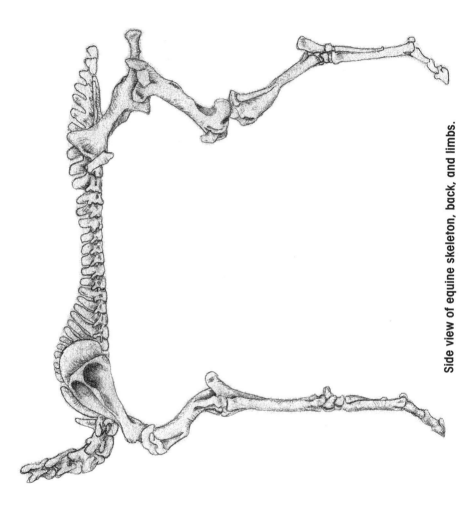

Side view of equine skeleton, back, and limbs.

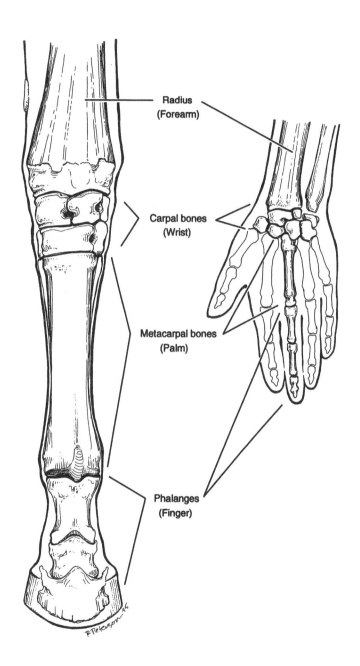

Radius
(Forearm)

Carpal bones
(Wrist)

Metacarpal bones
(Palm)

Phalanges
(Finger)

Equine-human anatomical comparison of front limb.

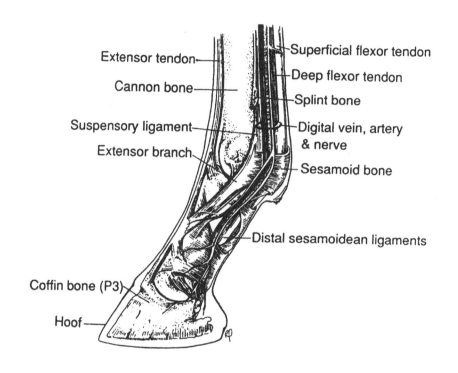

Extensor tendon

Cannon bone

Suspensory ligament

Extensor branch

Superficial flexor tendon

Deep flexor tendon

Splint bone

Digital vein, artery & nerve

Sesamoid bone

Distal sesamoidean ligaments

Coffin bone (P3)

Hoof

Tendons and ligaments of lower leg.

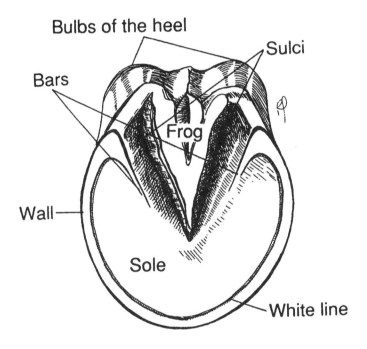

Bulbs of the heel

Sulci

Bars

Frog

Wall

Sole

White line

Ground surface view of hoof.

INDEX

RECOMMENDED READINGS

Adams, O.R. and Ted S. Stashak. Lameness in Horses. 4th ed. Philadelphia, Pa.: Lea & Febiger, 1987.

Brega, Julie. The Horse: the Foot. Shoeing & Lameness. London: J.A. Allen, 1995.

Gonzales, Tony. Proper Balance Movement: a Diary of Lameness. 1st ed. Manassas, Va.: REF Publishing, 1986.

Gray, Peter. Lameness. London: J.A. Allen, 1994.

Jones, William E. Sports Medicine for the Race Horse. Wildomar, Calif.: Veterinary Data, 1992.

King, Christine. Equine Lameness. Grand Prairie, Tex.: Equine Research, 1997.

Kinnish, Mary K., editor. Investigating Lameness: Sources of Leg Pain. Equus Stable Reference Guides. Gaithersburg, Md.: Fleet Street, 1988.

Lameness in Equine Practice, Compendium Collection. Trenton, N.J.: Veterinary Learning Systems, 1993.

Rooney, James. R., Rev. The Lame Horse, updated & expanded ed. Neenah, Wisc.: Russell Meerdink Co., 1997.

Stashak, Ted S. Horseowner's Guide to Lameness. Baltimore, Md.: Williams & Wilkins, 1996.

Vogel, Colin. The Complete Performance Horse: Preventive Medicine, Fitness, Feeding, Lameness. Newton Abbot, Devon: David & Charles, 1996.

Wyn-Jones, Geraint. Equine Lameness. Oxford: Blackwell Scientific Publications; Chicago: Distributors, USA, Year Book Medical Publishers, 1988.

Lameness sites on the Internet

The Horse Interactive: http://www.thehorse.com/

Hoofcare and Lameness: http://www.hoofcare.com/

American Association of Equine Practitioners Client Education articles: http://www.aaep.org/client.htm

The Equine Connection: The National AAEP Locator Service: http://www.getadvm.com/equcon.html

The Laminitis Page: http://www.olympus.net/personal/pvd/pvd.html

The Farrier and Hoofcare Resource Center: http://www. horseshoes.com/

Picture Credits

CHAPTER 1
Anne M. Eberhardt, 11; Barbara D. Livingston, 12; The Red Mile, 13.

CHAPTER 2
Anne M. Eberhardt, 16.

CHAPTER 3
Harold Campton, 28; Barbara D. Livingston, 34; Tom Hall, 34.

CHAPTER 4
Anne M. Eberhardt, 39, 43; *The Blood-Horse*, 44.

CHAPTER 5
Anne M. Eberhardt, 49-56.

CHAPTER 7
Anne M. Eberhardt, 91-93.

CHAPTER 8
Anne M. Eberhardt, 96, 97.

COVER/BOOK DESIGN — SUZANNE C. DEPP
ILLUSTRATIONS — ROBIN PETERSON
COVER PHOTOGRAPH — ANNE M. EBERHARDT

About the Author

Les Sellnow has been a lifelong journalist and horseman. He has competed in a variety of equine disciplines, ranging from combined training to cutting and from endurance racing to Western and English pleasure.

Through the years, Sellnow has been a student of proper foot and leg conformation and has written extensively on these subjects, as well as authoring articles in a number of equine publications on problems that can afflict a horse's feet and legs.

Les Sellnow As a journalist, he spent 22 years with the Brainerd (Minnesota) *Daily Dispatch*, rising from reporter to editor, winning state and national writing awards along the way. He and his wife, Linda, moved from Minnesota to Kentucky in 1984, where he served as editor of *National Show Horse* magazine and was a free-lance writer for *The Blood-Horse* magazine.

In 1994, the Sellnows moved to a ranch in the Wind River Valley, near Riverton, Wyoming. Sellnow is a regular contributor to *The Horse* and has had both fiction and non-fiction books published.